BEYOND AZTLAN

BEYOND AZTLAN

Ethnic Autonomy in Comparative Perspective

MARIO BARRERA

UNIVERSITY OF NOTRE DAME PRESS
NOTRE DAME   LONDON

Copyright Acknowledgments

The author and publisher are grateful to the following for allowing the use of excerpts from:

George Moseley, *The Party and the National Question in China* (Cambridge, MA: MIT Press, 1966). Reprinted by permission of the publisher.

Rodolfo Gonzales, *I Am Joaquin* (privately published, 1967). Reprinted by permission of the author.

Hurst Hannum and Richard Lillich, "The Concept of Autonomy in International Law," *The American Journal of International Law*, Vol. 74, No. 4 (October 1980). Reprinted by permission.

Library of Congress Cataloging-in-Publication Data

Barrera, Mario.
    Beyond Aztlan : ethnic autonomy in comparative perspective / Mario Barrera.
        p.   cm.
    Bibliography: p.
    Includes index.
    ISBN 0-275-92923-X (alk. paper)
    1. Mexican Americans—Ethnic identity.   2. Mexican Americans—Politics and government.   I. Title.
E184.M5B37   1988
305.8′6872′073—dc19   88-5432

Library of Congress Catalog Card Number: 88-5432
ISBN: 0-275-92923-X

First published in 1988

University of Notre Dame Press edition 1990

Praeger Publishers, One Madison Avenue, New York, NY 10010
A division of Greenwood Press, Inc.

Printed in the United States of America

For my son, Miguel Luis—

the next generation

Contents

Illustrations

FIGURES

TABLES

Preface

This book stems from my belief that Chicanos, like other ethnic minorities in the United States, are in the process of assimilating into the mainstream. It is a trend that I find disturbing, because it reduces cultural diversity in the society, and because I feel that Chicanos and others have not truly had a free choice in this matter. The "institutional dice" in the United States have always been loaded against cultural pluralism.

In seeking solutions to this problem, I have been led to look to other societies for alternative ways of ordering majority-minority relations. It is in this sense that this work is titled *Beyond Aztlan* (Aztlan being the mythic homeland of the Aztecs, a homeland located by contemporary Chicano nationalists in the U.S. Southwest). Too often we fall into the intellectual traps of thinking that our way is the only way and that what is, must be. Looking beyond our borders can be a way of opening our minds to the wide range of human possibilities.

During the years that I worked on this project, I was helped immeasurably by a great many people. My colleagues in the Department of Ethnic Studies at Berkeley have been a constant source of encouragement; I would particularly like to thank Carlos Munoz, Alex Saragoza, Larry Trujillo, Ron Takaki, Terry Wilson, and Margarita Melville. I also received much help from the following staff members: Rosa Johnson, Maria Hernandez, Ana Coronado, Magali Zuniga, and librarian Lillian Castillo Speed.

I am indebted to the following for reading and commenting on earlier versions of some of this work: Mario Garcia, Ben Marquez, Rudy Torres, Daniel Latouche, Roxanne Dunbar Ortiz, Renato Rosaldo, Jose Limon, Louisa Schein, Michael Banton, David Gutierrez, Linda Kahn, Carlos Cortes, Rodolfo Rocha, Isidro Ortiz, and my students in my graduate seminar in comparative ethnic relations. Richard Llata was a great help with the China section.

The word-processing and editorial skills of Susan Barrera have been an invaluable help to me. I also owe much to the encouragement and support of Dan Moreno, Marilyn Mulford, Frances Hernandez, and Wendy Hyman.

Work on this book was aided by fellowships from the National Research Council, the University of California, and the Smithsonian Institution.

I

THE HISTORY OF CHICANO ETHNIC GOALS

1

Introduction: Goals, Dilemmas, and Autonomy

Aztlan, according to legend, was the ancestral homeland of the Aztecs. It was the land they had left in journeying southward to found Tenochtitlán, the center of their new civilization, now the site of Mexico City (Chavez, 1984; Smith, 1984). Few people in the United States were familiar with the concept of Aztlan until Chicano Movement activists of the 1960s revived it and proclaimed it a central symbol of Chicano nationalist ideology. The rediscovery of Aztlan can be traced to a specific event, the Chicano National Liberation Youth Conference that took place in Denver in 1969. There, Colorado political activist Rodolfo "Corky" Gonzales put forth a brief but influential political document entitled El Plan de Aztlan. In that statement can be found many of the key issues dealt with in this book.

The Plan de Aztlan argued that nationalism must be the key to organizing Chicanos to struggle against racism and exploitation. The focus was to be on unifying all Chicanos to gain control of their communities and of the institutions that affected their daily lives. Community control in turn would allow more equitable social policies and greater economic and political equality, and would give the people the means to safeguard their distinctive cultural identity (see Chapter 4).

While El Plan de Aztlan stated the goal of ethnic nationalism in a forceful manner, the exact form that nationalism should take was nowhere spelled out. The resulting ambiguity was to remain an aspect of the Chicano Movement throughout its short but eventful trajectory. Specific political actions such as the formation of a third party and the organizing of movements to gain control of city councils and boards of education were undertaken in the following years, but a clear statement of the eventual relationship of Chicanos to the political system of the United States never emerged.

The present book is thus an attempt to sort out some critical issues that were left unresolved during that period. I have chosen to begin by examining the long political road that led to Denver. In Chapters 2 through 5, I present a history of the development of Chicano ethnic goals, beginning with their origins in the nineteenth century and continuing through the Chicano Movement to the present time. In these chapters, I argue that two types of goals have characterized Chicano political history, *equality* and *community*. The first of these goals refers to economic, social, and political equality between Chicanos and the mainstream white, or "Anglo," population. The second involves the maintenance of a cohesive and culturally distinct communal identity. The relationship between the two goals has been problematic, and some organizations have stressed one over the other. In most organizations, both goals have existed in a state of dynamic tension.

The second section of the book can be seen as having its point of departure in another political statement that was published shortly before El Plan de Aztlan. This particular document took the form of an epic poem by the same Rodolfo "Corky" Gonzales, titled *I Am Joaquin*, or "Yo Soy Joaquin." The poem begins with the following passage:

> I am Joaquin,
> Lost in a world of confusion,
> Caught up in a whirl of an
>   Anglo society,
> Confused by the rules,
> Scorned by attitudes,
> Suppressed by manipulations,
> And destroyed by modern society.
> My fathers
>   Have lost the economic battle

and won
    the struggle of cultural survival (Gonzales, 1967:3).

In Chapter 6, I present evidence that for the sons and daughters of those fathers, the opposite is closer to the truth. While the economic battle is far from being won, significant progress in the occupational status of Chicanos has taken place since World War II. The "struggle of cultural survival," on the other hand, is rapidly being lost. Indeed, the limited economic and educational gains that have been made in recent decades have had the effect of accelerating the assimilation process. The results can be seen most dramatically in the overwhelming loss of fluency in Spanish by the third generation, but it can be seen as well in the trend toward residential dispersion and the rising rate of intermarriage.

These processes have created a dilemma for Chicanos that is rarely acknowledged in public debate or in statements by leading political organizations. The focus continues to be on achieving greater economic mobility for Mexican Americans, and yet the very successes of that effort, limited as they may be, serve to undercut the distinctive collective identity that has so frequently been articulated as a political goal. Are there solutions to this dilemma? Does the achievement of economic equality in a multiethnic society necessarily mean that minority groups must take on the cultural identity of the majority? Thinking about these questions led me to take a new and somewhat unexpected direction. I decided that it would be useful to look at other multiethnic societies to see how other countries have dealt with majority-minority relations. I did this in full recognition that each society is unique but that certain commonalities can be found in all societies where different cultural communities coexist. In my own mind, I was not looking for a "correct" model to emulate, but rather for the raw material of ideas from other societies' experiences that could be useful in constructing our own "guiding image" of a future, more just and more equitable United States (Gretler and Mandl, 1973).

In my opinion, political movements too often act and think in isolation, as if the entire world can be found within the political boundaries of their own country. A look at other situations can have the effect of stimulating thought about alternatives, and lead to the realization that there are solutions that have long since been implemented in other countries, although they are not even discussed in the United States. It is my feeling that, intellectually, it is time to "go comparative." I also feel that it is important at times to think in the longer run and to propose fundamental solutions that may seem quite unrealistic and even utopian in the short run. Political groups and political activists are forced to operate in a world of continuous crisis and immediate problems requiring responses now. Those of us in the universities, conversely, have the opportunity and the obligation to look at trends and to create scenarios in a longer time frame.

Through a long process, which I will not try to describe here, I eventually focused on a group of four countries: Canada (Quebec), China, Switzerland, and Nicaragua. The description of their experiences and their solutions can be found in Chapters 7 and 8. Although it may seem at first glance to be a somewhat odd grouping, these four countries do have some things in common: all are multiethnic societies, and all have worked out internal arrangements that might be described as a pluralistic accommodation, one in which the most significant minority groups are recognized as having important rights as groups. All of these countries explicitly declare in their constitutions and their laws that they are multicultural and multilingual in nature.

In addition, all of them have evolved a system of governance in which the minority ethnic groups have achieved a certain degree of political control over their historic territories. In the case of China, a system called regional autonomy has been in place since the 1950s. Under that system, each minority group has certain designated territories in which special provisions are made to safeguard its economic and cultural rights. In Canada, the largest minority ethnic group, the French-speaking Quebecois, have managed to gain political control over one of Canada's major provinces, and have also won important recognition of their cultural rights from the national government. The Swiss case is perhaps the most remarkable example of a pluralistic accommodation that exists anywhere. It is the culmination of a social process that has been underway for centuries and that has resulted in the identification of the various cantons (similar to provinces or states) with the major Swiss cultural groups. In the case of Nicaragua, the move toward their own particular brand of regional autonomy is very recent, dating only from 1984. It is of particular interest because of the important political experiment that has been underway in that country since the 1979 revolution, and because they are dealing with minorities that are racially as well as ethnically distinct. Following very diverse paths, then, all of these societies have arrived at an accommodation based on institutional arrangements that allow a significant degree of ethnic autonomy on a regional basis. This type of accommodation provides a framework for working out questions of equality while preserving cultural distinctiveness and avoiding separation.

In the concluding chapter, I rework and reconsider the material from the comparative chapters and draw out the implications for the United States, and especially for the case of Chicanos. Is it possible to achieve a reconciliation of the goals of community and equality in this country, achieving social justice without sacrificing cultural diversity? I argue that it is, but only with a major and long-term political effort, and a major reorientation of political thinking on the part of both minority and majority. The first step would be to gain an explicit legal recognition of a very obvious social reality—that the United States is in fact a multicultural and multilingual country. Once that had been accomplished, the way would be open for a discussion of some form of ethnic regional autonomy in this country. Although consideration of such a solution might seem very abstract at this historical moment, changing population patterns might make it seem less so in the future.

Most of the terms I use in this work are explained in the text. However, I would like to comment briefly on the use of the term "Chicano." Often this term is used to refer specifically to people of Mexican descent in the United States whose political consciousness was formed during the Chicano Movement period, roughly 1968–1973. People who self-consciously designate themselves as Chicano generally use it as a way of expressing cultural pride and an assertive, if not defiant, political position. When I use the term in this manner, its meaning will be clear from the context. Throughout most of the work, however, the term "Chicano" is used as a synonym for Mexican Americans in general.

2

The Emergence of Chicano Ethnic Goals

People of Mexican descent became a United States ethnic group as a result of the Mexican American War, 1846–1848, which ended with the forced cession of half of Mexico's territory. The Treaty of Guadalupe Hidalgo allowed the former Mexican citizens living in the ceded territory to move to what was left of Mexico, or to stay put and become U.S. citizens. The entry of this group into the United States as a conquered people exerted a profound influence on their subsequent history.

THE NINETEENTH CENTURY: POLITICS IN A PERIOD OF DECLINE

The major development in the second half of the nineteenth century that shaped the Chicano experience was the relative decline in the fortunes of Chicanos of all classes in the new American Southwest. The pace of this decline was dictated by the speed with which the United States was able to incorporate this area into the framework of its political economy.

The penetration of the vast Southwest by the new economic order was uneven, taking place rapidly in northern California with the Gold Rush, and in Texas, where there were already extensive Anglo settlements. In southern California, the pace of the change-over picked up in the 1870s with the arrival of the intercontinental railroads. In New Mexico, Arizona, and southern Colorado, the transformation was more gradual but nonetheless profound. Given the uneven rate of penetration, it comes as no surprise that the Chicano response was also uneven, as was the rate of change of the traditional frontier Mexican social and political relationships in the area.

The Chicano downward mobility that accompanied this capitalist transformation took various forms. The struggle for control of the land was over fairly quickly in northern California with the dispossession of the wealthy "Californio" elite. In northern New Mexico, that struggle continues to this day. The process that Alberto Camarillo (1979) has labeled "proletarianization"—the conversion of Mexican peasants, small farmers, artisans, and others into Chicano wage workers—followed a similar path. In the political realm, the "Californio" elite had been effectively displaced before the end of the century (Pitt, 1966). The other large and well-established "Hispano" elite of New Mexico was able to hold on to a degree of power longer because of the greater percentage of Chicano residents there.

Throughout the Southwest, the Chicano political response was one of reacting to this downward mobility in a defensive posture. This reaction, however, took different forms in different areas and time periods. Social banditry was one such form, especially in California and Texas. That the individual revolts of men like Gregorio Cortez, Joaquin Murieta, Jacinto Trevino, and Tiburcio Vasquez had broad support in the Chicano community has been demonstrated through the passing on of their exploits in legends and corridos (Rosenbaum, 1981:53–61; Castillo and Camarillo, 1973; Cortes, 1971; Rocha, 1981). At times, spontaneous acts of defensive violence took on the proportions of a full-scale insurrection, as in 1859, when Juan Cortina mobilized a force in the Lower Rio Grande Valley of Texas that required the intervention of the U.S. Army.

The landed elite in California, New Mexico, and Arizona responded by entering the electoral arena and building a political base on a Chicano constituency. Demographic realities doomed these efforts before the end of the century, with the partial exception of New Mexico. There the "ricos" were able to maintain effective political machines because of the numerical superiority of the Chicano population and the traditional ties that had existed between

"ricos" and "pobres" for generations (Fincher, 1950:103). This Hispano elite pursued their interests through the Republican party
and the various "rings" that dominated New Mexican territorial
politics of that period, in alliance with wealthy Anglos who were
ultimately the dominant partners in the coalitions (Zeleny, 1944:208–
9; Holmes, 1967:Chapter 2).

Social banditry and limited insurrection, on the one hand, and
electoral politics, on the other, were thus the major types of Chicano political response in the nineteenth century. The politics of
the period were heavily influenced by the continuation of the pre-
capitalist social and economic relations that had existed in the area
before the Mexican American War. The existence of a class structure that featured a wealthy Chicano elite and a much larger number of poor Chicanos dependent on them sharply limited the political possibilities. The elite was more interested in defending its
own interests than in defining a broader "community" interest with
a traditionally subservient class. Much of the Chicano upper class
identified with the new Anglo elite, and played by the rules of the
political game in hopes of holding on to some of their declining
fortunes. As this traditional class structure slowly evaporated, and
as a small but influential Chicano middle class emerged alongside
a growing Chicano working class, the more complex political responses of the twentieth century became possible.

Toward the end of the nineteenth century, one of the more in-
teresting Chicano political movements took place in northern New
Mexico, where the traditional class relations were historically weak.
Here, the Chicano response to expropriation took the form of "Las
Gorras Blancas" (The White Caps), active in northern New Mexico
from 1889 to 1891.

Las Gorras Blancas operated in an area where most of the land
grants had been awarded to communities rather than to individuals. The general pattern was for members of the community to be
assigned small plots for their households and for subsistence farm-
ing, with the bulk of the land to be used communally for grazing
and gathering timber. Under this concept, the land belonged to
the community as a whole and could not be alienated without the
consent of the entire community. Anglo ranching companies moving into the area, however, made it a practice to purchase interests
from the original grantees and then to fence off a proportional amount

of the grant land for their exclusive use, including the communal property. In essence, they refused to recognize the concept of communal lands (Schlesinger, 1971:95; Rosenbaum, 1981:101).

As this process unfolded on the Las Vegas Grant in San Miguel County, community residents challenged the practice in court, but despite some successes, were unable to reverse the process. As a result, bands of Chicano masked riders began resorting to direct action in 1889, cutting fences and burning the property of the offending ranchers. Although the main targets of their actions were Anglo, some Hispanos were also erecting fences and thus became objects of Las Gorras Blancas' wrath (Schlesinger, 1971:98). That the White Caps had the support of local residents was made clear from a citizens' meeting called by the authorities in August of 1890. The overwhelming bulk of the citizens who turned out supported Las Gorras Blancas (Romero, 1981:15).

Las Gorras Blancas put out a platform in March of 1890. Among other things, the platform states:

Our purpose is to protect the rights and interests of the people in general and especially those of the helpless classes.

We want the Las Vegas Grant settled to the benefit of all concerned, and this we hold is the entire community within the Grant.

We want no "land grabbers" or obstructionists of any sort to interfere. . . .

The people are suffering from the effects of partisan "bossism" and these bosses had better quietly hold their peace. The people have been persecuted and hauled about in every which way to satisfy their caprices. . . .

If the fact that we are law-abiding citizens is questioned, come out to our houses and see the hunger and desolation we are suffering; and "this" is the result of the deceitful and corrupt methods of "bossism" (Weber, 1973:235–36).

Beyond these general statements, and what can be read into their activities, Las Gorras Blancas did not set forth an explicit set of goals. Their aspirations appear to have been purely defensive and conserving of the old order, as well as localistic in their orientation (Larson, 1975:176).

Historically, Las Gorras Blancas are linked to two other organizations. In their origins, there were ties to the Knights of Labor, a national anticapitalist organization of workers. The Knights lent support to the original lawsuit involving the Las Vegas Grant, and two of the major organizers of Las Gorras Blancas, the Herrera brothers, were active members of the Knights (Schlesinger, 1971:103; Larson, 1975:178). The involvement of the Knights of Labor, however, was more out of anticapitalist and antimonopolist sentiment than out of sympathy for the concept of communal land grants, and they disassociated themselves from the nightriding of Las Gorras Blancas.

Las Gorras Blancas in turn fed into El Partido del Pueblo Unido, formed in 1890 as a coalition of Las Gorras Blancas leaders, aspiring Hispano Democratic party activists, Anglo Knights of Labor, dissaffected Hispano Republicans, and others (Rosenbaum, 1981:126–27). Running on a platform emphasizing the land issue and opposition to the "bossism" of the notorious New Mexico "rings," the Partido enjoyed some initial success but quickly degenerated into factionalism. Electoral politics thus became a dead end as far as the interests of poor Hispanos were concerned. The establishment in 1891 of the Court of Private Land Claims in New Mexico to handle the issue of the land grants also served to divert energy from direct action to established procedures.

THE MUTUALISTA PERIOD

Mutual aid societies, also known as fraternal insurance societies, have been more important in Chicano communities historically than is usually realized. It is no exaggeration to say that after the family, the mutualistas were the most important social organization among Chicanos from the late nineteenth century to the 1930s. As Paul Taylor noted in one of his famous studies, "These societies represent the only continuous organized life among the Mexicans in which the initiative comes wholly from the Mexicans themselves" (Taylor, 1928:45).

Mutual aid societies were not, of course, found only in Chicano communities. Similar organizations were established in the nineteenth century in many countries and among many nationalities in the United States. According to a standard interpretation, these societies arose among newly urbanized groups who felt the need for some form of organization to replace the extended kinship and community ties that had provided support in rural areas (Briegel, 1974:2–8). Many Chicanos were immigrants in a double sense, from Mexico to the United States and from rural to urban settings. It was in the urban areas that these societies became most popular among Chicanos, and particularly in those towns that served as trading or commercial centers. Interestingly enough, they were slow to develop in northern New Mexico, where the traditional communities remained viable for a longer period (ibid., 67).

The original rationale for Chicano mutual-aid societies was to cover funeral expenses upon the death of one of their members, expenses that were serious burdens for poor families. As the societies evolved, however, they developed more general-purpose life insurance coverage. Most of them also offered a wide range of social activities, including dances, barbecues, and celebrations of Mexican patriotic holidays, and were an important source of social cohesion in the community. A few provided other services, such as employment agencies, adult education, health clinics, and libraries (Hernandez, 1979:155–57).

The largest and most successful of the Chicano mutualistas was the Alianza Hispano-Americana, founded in Tucson, Arizona, in 1894. The origins of this organization are of some interest, for, as Briegel notes:

> The Alianza . . . was not organized simply to provide social activities and low cost life insurance for its members. It was also organized in an attempt to preserve the prestige and influence of Tucson community leaders of Mexican descent against changing circumstances. The Alianza conducted a death benefit program, social events and, although not overtly, political activities.
>
> The formation of a defense organization such as the Alianza seemed necessary to people of Mexican descent in Tucson in 1894 (Briegel, 1974:91).

Here, we see some continuities with the politics of decline. In the case of southern Arizona, it happened that the interests of the Chicano elite in creating a political base to help withstand the Anglo challenge coincided with the need of the Chicano working class for some form of social insurance. At that time, commercial insurance companies offered relatively expensive policies and considered minorities to be poor risks (ibid., 55).

The mid–1890s were also a period in which American nativism was on the rise. The Panic of 1893 had aggravated tensions in the general society, and local Tucson bigots had organized a local chapter of the American Protective Association, the most influential nativist group of that period. Added to the shaky economic fortunes of the Chicano elite, then, were Anglo nativist attacks on Chicano rich and poor alike (ibid., 35–38).

The Alianza was broad in the scope of its membership, with the elite in leadership positions and the poor as rank-and-file members. It welcomed newer immigrants as well as the more established Chicano residents, a pattern that was true of most mutualistas of the period (Briegel, 1974:12, 41; Hernandez, 1979:63–67). Camarillo (1979:148–49), however, has described a mutual-aid society in the Santa Barbara area of California, the Club Mexicano Independencia, which restricted membership to citizens of Mexico.

The mutualistas tended to put heavy stress on their Mexican heritage. According to Hernandez, "Chicano benefit associations were not generally concerned with the assimilation of the Mexican population into the dominant culture" (Hernandez, 1979:7). The Alianza followed this practice, always using Spanish in its proceedings and basing its elaborate rituals on Mexican culture and heroes, at least through the 1930s (Briegel, 1974:153).

Soon after its beginnings in Tucson, the Alianza expanded to other trading centers and mining towns in Arizona, and then into California. By the 1910s, it had expanded into Texas and parts of New Mexico. Some lodges were even formed in the northern part of Mexico, although these eventually split off to form a separate organization. In 1922, the Alianza's total membership was about 6,000, and by 1929 had grown to over 13,000, partly as a result of continued high immigration from Mexico. It reached the peak of its membership in 1939, with 17,366 formally enrolled (ibid., 84, 89, 126). By the late 1930s, about half of its membership was located in California, with the largest concentration in the greater Los Angeles area.

After the 1930s, the Alianza entered a slow period of decline, eventually dwindling into bankruptcy in the 1960s. Several factors have been cited to explain the declining fortunes of the Alianza and other mutualistas after the 1930s. One is the greater availability of government social security programs beginning with the New Deal. Another is the greater competition offered by commercial insurance companies in recent decades. The social and entertainment value of the mutual aid societies also decreased with the growth of the mass media and the greater mobility offered by postwar society. Finally, it appears that the development of more specialized Chicano organizations after 1940, including specifically political organizations, drew potential members away and served in some ways to narrow the focus of the mutualistas. It is perhaps also true that the greater employment opportunities available to Chicanos during and after World War II improved their economic position and made them less dependent on the low insurance rates offered by the mutual aid societies (Briegel, 1974:143ff, 202; Hernandez, 1979:252).

It is possible to say some things about the goals and aspirations of the mutual aid societies, while keeping in mind that there was variation from society to society and over time. The central concern of the mutualistas during their golden age appears to have been the social cohesion of the Chicano community. Membership in a mutual aid society provided a kind of social safety net, to use a current term, that helped preserve the integrity and the peace of mind of the working-class Chicano family. At the same time, the social activities that were very important to most mutualistas afforded a focus for community interaction that was provided by no other mechanism (Camarillo, 1979:153–54).

Hernandez has described the feeling of cohesiveness described here as a form of nationalism, although with a special flavor:

The nationalism of Mexicans, Mexican Americans, or Chicanos was not the same thing . . . as the simple love of country. . . . The nature of their nationalism took an interesting form. It tended to transcend geographic lines. While the term "Chicano community" frequently refers to a physical concentration of individuals at a place bound by culture or lifestyle, it often refers also to the people identified as members of the Mexican ethnic group. That is, nationalism was somewhat of a mystical idea embodied not so much in the state as in the spirit or soul of the group. Chicano nationalism was a mutualista spiritual principle that advanced the concept of la Raza as an organic unit, members of which shared a rich heritage of memories and a heroic past (Hernandez, 1983:90).

Interestingly enough, that mystical feeling of unity was usually not enough to maintain the attempts that were made from time to time to form broad umbrella organizations of mutualistas. Local attachments were sufficiently strong to make each mutual aid society the primary focus of activity. The historian Juan Garcia has echoed many of these same themes for mutual aid societies formed in the Midwest:

Although mutual aid societies were seldom, if ever, openly defiant, they nonetheless were a symbol of the determination of *Mexicanos* to retain their values and culture . . . The true importance of mutual aid societies which sprang up in the Midwest lay in the social function which they served. They brought the community together by sponsoring dances, holiday celebrations, funerals, weddings, and baptisms. . . . Furthermore, the mutual aid societies were very nationalistic. They encouraged their members to resist assimilation and citizenship status in the United States. Their goal in places like Chicago, Detroit, Lansing, and other midwestern communities was to perpetuate the allegiance of *Mexicanos* to their homeland. To accomplish this it was necessary to have members retain their language and culture. . . . The Mexican/Mexican-American communities played active roles in helping to maintain a sense of solidarity among people of Mexican descent. Even the names of the organizations were designed so as to foster pride in the mestizo-Indian heritage of Mexico. Thus, names emerged for organizations such as *La Sociedad Jose Maria Morelos, La Sociedad Mutualista Cuauhtemoc*, and *La Sociedad Mutualista Benito Juarez* (Garcia, 1982:94).

After 1940, it appears that at least some of the leadership of the Alianza Hispano-Americana adopted a more assimilationist stance. The president of the society during the 1940s, Sedillo, sponsored programs that stressed patriotism and civic duty, and operated on the assumption that Chicanos could advance in American society through hard work (Briegel, 1974:149–53).

The major focus of the mutualistas was never on overcoming discrimination and fighting for equality within the broader society, although this type of goal did play a role for some of the groups in some time periods. The Alianza, for example, embarked on an ambitious civil rights program during the 1950s. Alianza staff lawyers took on issues involving public school desegregation, access to public facilities such as swimming pools, and discrimination in the employment of Chicanos by government agencies. During this same decade the Alianza also helped form the American Council on Spanish Speaking People, which took on similar issues (Briegel, 1974:167–73; 153; Hernandez, 1983:45ff). The mutualistas also supported union-organizing efforts at times, although not consistently. For example, mutual aid societies backed union struggles among Chicanos in the Clifton-Morenci area of Arizona in the early 1900s (Briegel, 1974:10–11; Hernandez, 1983:36–44). Another group, the Confederacion de Sociedades Mexicanas, based in Los Angeles, served as an organizer for unions of Chicano workers that subsequently formed the Confederacion de Union Obreros Mexicanos (Hernandez, 1979:153).

A case study of a southern California mutual-aid society in the 1970s, however, found most of its members favoring a narrow concept of the group's functions. Most members of the Sociedad Progresista Mexicana did not see the society as an appropriate place to deal with community and political issues and were generally conservative in their outlook (Hernandez, 1983:111–21).

Plan of San Diego

A series of events that took place during the mutualista period deserves some mention here. In January of 1915, a document entitled The Plan of San Diego was discovered by U.S. authorities in the Lower Rio Grande Valley of Texas. This was the first of a number of "Plans" that were written by or attributed to Chicanos. The Plan of San Diego purported to be a manifesto for a popular insurrection of Chicanos in the southwestern states, with the goal of establishing an independent republic. It further stipulated that at some future date, said republic might be annexed to Mexico (Gomez-Quiñones 1970:128–30). The document was supposed to have been conceived and signed in San Diego, Texas.

During the later part of 1915, a series of raids convulsed southern Texas, most originating in Mexico. The raids had a number of consequences, including the out-migration of a large number of south Texas residents, an increase of racial tensions in the area, and the severe straining of United States–Mexico relations, already tense because of fallout from the Mexican Revolution (1910–

1920). That the raids were related to the Plan of San Diego seemed increasingly evident as they gathered force.

The Plan of San Diego has been subjected to various interpretations. One is that the plan was indeed what it claimed to be, an insurrectionary movement on the part of Chicanos who had been pushed to the limit by Anglo racism, particularly in Texas. Another explanation, favored by a number of historians, is that the plan was instigated by Victoriano Huerta, the deposed former Mexican president who was trying to regain power. In this interpretation, the Plan of San Diego was intended to divert the attention of U.S. authorities from Huerta's use of south Texas as a staging ground for an invasion of Mexico (see, for example, Gerlach, 1968).

A more recent and more thoroughly documented study, however, presents a strong case for a third interpretation. In this interpretation, the Plan of San Diego was implemented by the Mexican politician Venustiano Carranza, at that point contesting with Villa and Zapata for supreme power in Mexico (Harris and Sadler, 1978). Carranza's forces controlled the border area from which most of the raids originated. Carranza's motivation was to apply pressure to U.S. authorities for official American recognition for his regime, thus strengthening his hand in Mexico. Mexican Americans, in this scheme, were seen as a convenient fifth column who provided fertile ground for mobilization because of the long-standing racial tensions in the Southwest. When Carranza did in fact receive U.S. recognition, the raids ceased, to be revived briefly in 1916 as a response to General Pershing's punitive expedition into Mexico (Harris and Sadler, 1978:392–402).

The Chicano historian Rodolfo Rocha, after a review of the events in question and the various interpretations, concludes as follows:

> While it is popular to see the incidents as the implementation of the *Plan de San Diego*, it may not be historically accurate to do so. Poverty, the personal gains to be made by individuals trading with Mexican factions, and the *Carrancista* need for American recognition all were factors contributing to the uprising. Charges that *Carrancista* troops comprised some of the raiders, though accurate to some degree, are inaccurate if they are extended to include all. Carranza's contribution to the forays came in the unofficial support he gave the marauders by allowing them to take sanctuary in Mexico (Rocha, 1981:321).

Thus, even after a number of studies, the Plan de San Diego remains ambiguous in many ways, and its significance unclear. It is still difficult to gauge the extent of Chicano participation in the plan and the raids or to judge the degree to which Chicano political aspirations were reflected in those events.

CONCLUSION

In the difficult period that followed the Mexican American War, the Chicano response was defensive in nature. Chicanos attempted to hold on to what resources they could and to reach an accommodation with the new social order. In so doing, they tried as best they could to maintain the integrity of their communities and their group cultural identity. The preservation of a cohesive and culturally distinct community identity can be seen as the first of the ethnic goals to be historically defined by Chicanos. This is referred to as the communitarian goal in later sections of this book.

3

The Shift to Equality

There were two major events during the 1910s that had important consequences for the situation of Chicanos and for their political and community organizations.

The Mexican Revolution, which lasted the entire decade, was a stimulus to the first large waves of Mexican immigration to the United States, although a number of other conditions in Mexico also contributed. This large-scale immigration, accelerating in the 1920s, led to the growth of Chicano/Mexicano communities and expanded the base for the mutualistas and other groups. At the same time, the revolution spawned the Plan of San Diego and the border raids discussed in the previous chapter. These raids and the fear and confusion that they created in Texas led to a massive backlash against Mexican and Chicano residents of that state and resulted in a greatly increased level of official and unofficial harassment and lynchings.

Carranza's policy had succeeded brilliantly, but at a terrible cost to Mexican-Americans; by the fall of 1915, south Texas was on the verge of a race war. For all the turmoil they had caused, the raiders had inflicted surprisingly few casualties: eleven soldiers killed and seventeen wounded, and six civilians killed and eight wounded, according to official figures. But they had triggered a backlash of massive proportions. The Anglo minority, who had come to take the Plan of San Diego very seriously, viewed themselves as engaged in a struggle for survival against the Mexicans. Anglo fear had manifested itself in a wave of summary killings by rangers, local officers, and citizens (Harris and Sadler, 1978:390).

The other major event of the decade was World War I, which stimulated the economy and led to greater employment opportunities for Chicanos in and out of the Southwest, and encouraged greater immigration.

These events, together with internal changes taking place within the Chicano community, were to lead to the creation of a number of Chicano organizations with a radically different definition of appropriate ethnic goals.

THE ORDER OF SONS OF AMERICA AND THE LEAGUE OF UNITED LATIN AMERICAN CITIZENS

The Order of Sons of America (OSA) was organized in San Antonio in 1921 by a group of community leaders. Its characteristics reflected the situation and climate of opinion that had been created in the preceding decade. Hernandez (1979:129) states that the group was conceived as a benefit fraternal society and that it was made up of professionals and white collar workers. In a striking departure from tradition, however, the group was restricted to U.S. citizens, native born or naturalized. From what we know of this important and little-studied group, it also differed from the mutual aid societies in being more explicitly political in its orientation, putting its emphasis on gaining equal access to and equal treatment from public institutions. Its goals are listed by Guzman as including the following:

1. Elimination of racial prejudice
2. Equality before the law
3. Improved educational opportunities
4. A reasonable share of the political representation in the affairs of the community, State and Nation (Guzman, 1966:375).

The group also "placed great emphasis on learning the English language and the acquisition of naturalization papers" (ibid., 375).

Its notable victories included gaining the right of Chicanos to serve on juries in the Corpus Christi area and removing barriers to public accommodations (Hernandez, 1979:141). No evidence has come to light, however, of directly partisan activity on the part of the group.

The orientation of the OSA is understandable when put in context. The wave of Mexican immigration coming into Texas had led to a fear on the part of middle class and white collar Chicanos that they would be swamped by the new arrivals, and that their own precarious status would be undermined if the dominant Anglo population failed to differentiate them from the working-class immigrants (Woods, 1949:21). The creation of the Order of Sons of America thus appears to be the first organizational sign of a diverging identity between the more established Chicano residents and the newer Mexicano arrivals. The apprehensions of middle class Chicanos had undoubtedly been significantly bolstered by the wave of paranoia that swept Texas following the Plan of San Diego raids, as well as the 1920–1921 pressures for the repatriation of Mexican immigrants. World War I patriotism may also have played a role here, and the rampant nativism of the period certainly did. By stressing citizenship and the mastery of English—and indeed in its very title—the Sons of America sought to reassure Texas Anglos that they could be trusted to be loyal and upstanding citizens. It is not surprising that the Mexican nationalist tone of the mutualistas is missing here.

By 1929, the OSA had formed seven councils in different Texas cities, but in that year, a split within the organization led its two largest chapters, San Antonio and Corpus Christi, to join in an effort to form a new group in Texas, the League of United Latin American Citizens (LULAC). This group, which Sandoval (1979a:32) refers to as "the" Chicano organization from 1929 to 1945, is also seen by many as the quintessentially assimilationist Chicano group.

LULAC originated as an effort to unite several existing Chicano organizations in Texas, chief among them being the OSA, the Knights of America, and the League of Latin American Citizens. From its initial Texas base, LULAC spread to New Mexico in the 1930s and then to Colorado, California, and Arizona (Garza, 1951:4, 10; Sandoval, 1979a:11–12, 20–21). A 1979 article lists it as having 100,000 members in thirty-four states, making it the largest national Latino organization. However, the same article points out that its membership has been stagnant since 1960 and that it has failed to attract youth in recent decades (Sandoval, 1979b:30). More recently, the LULACs have stressed the formation of youth chapters to counteract this trend.

LULAC from its inception was primarily a middle class organization and like OSA, limited in its membership to U.S. citizens of Mexican origin. It was not intended as a mass or grass-roots organization but rather as a cadre of activists (Weeks, 1929:272). In 1948, its membership was opened up to sympathetic non-Chicano citizens (Garza, 1951:22), and presently, it is possible for non-citizens to join as well.

From a contemporary perspective, it does seem that the LULACs went somewhat overboard in their attempt to make their point. English was its official language, and as Sandoval points out, it was modeled on U.S. organizations rather than Mexican groups (Sandoval, 1929a:3). The George Washington Prayer was, and still is, its official prayer, and the American flag its official emblem (Garza, 1951:8–9). The LULAC Code says, in part:

Respect your citizenship and preserve it; honor your country, maintain its tradition in the spirit of its citizens and embody yourself into its culture and civilization (ibid., 19).

The LULAC Aims and Purposes states, in part:

As Loyal Citizens of the United States of America . . . [w]e accept that it is not only the privilege but also the obligation of every member of this organization to uphold and defend the rights and duties vested in every American Citizen by the letter and the spirit of the law of the land.

As members of a democratic society, we recognize our civic duties and responsibilities and we propose . . . to foster the acquisition and facile use of the official language of our country that we may thereby equip ourselves and our families for the fullest enjoyment of our rights and privileges and the efficient discharge of our duties and obligations to this, our country (ibid., 20).

It is notable and a telling comment on the Texas political climate that despite their patriotic rhetoric and assimilationist pretensions, the LULACs met fierce resistance when they tried to organize

Chicanos in a number of Texas communities, being red-baited and even run out of town on occasion (Sandoval, 1979a:17–19). While LULAC claimed that it was a nonpolitical organization, and shunned partisan politics, it involved itself in a wide variety of antidiscrimination activities. School integration was one of its goals, and the LULAC News reported on one victory in the following terms:

JUDGE RICE'S DECISION . . . THE AMERICAN SPIRIT

Democratic, "Melting-Pot" assimilation has scored another victory over prejudicial segregation in the Federal court of Judge Ben H. Rice at Austin. In a representative class action applying to a minority of some 190 Texas school districts with objectionable educational practices, Judge Rice held:

School districts may not segregate pupils of Latin American descent, except in separate classes on the same campus, in the first grade only, to overcome language difficulties. . . . State aid must be withheld from districts refusing to comply (quoted in Garza, 1951:32).

The LULACs also entered into battle over access to public accommodations, exclusion of Chicanos from juries, discriminatory voting practices such as the poll tax, better working conditions for migrant laborers and Mexican braceros (contract laborers), and employment discrimination in World War II defense industry (Sandoval, 1979a:53–60).

The LULACs, then, even more than the OSA, represented a significant turnaround in Chicano organizing, with far greater attention to issues of socioeconomic and political equality on U.S. terms and very little concern with issues of community cohesion as such.

THE MEXICAN AMERICAN MOVEMENT

Another organization began in California in the 1930s, originally in the form of annual "Mexican Youth Conferences" and later as the Mexican American Movement (MAM). Whereas the social base of the OSA and LULAC was in the Chicano small business and independent professional class of south Texas, MAM sprang from a group of California college students with professional aspirations.

The original Mexican Youth Conferences were organized by the Young Men's Christian Association (YMCAs) as part of their outreach youth work. Along with other religious and social-work organizations, the YMCA was concerned with Americanizing immigrant youth and saving them from the pitfalls of radical ideologies (Munoz, 1981:13). The first of the conferences took place in southern California in 1934 and attracted Chicano youth from the high schools and colleges. The conferences stressed education as the key to upward mobility, hard work and the Protestant ethic, and Americanism (ibid., 15).

Within a short period of time, a leadership group emerged from the Chicano youth, consisting primarily of college students. This group established a newsletter called the *Mexican American Voice* in 1939 and a number of youth clubs that functioned in conjunction with the conferences (Munoz, 1981:10, 18; Gomez-Quiñones, 1978:10). These clubs were open to U.S. citizens only. In 1942, the same leadership group, many of them now graduates, initiated the Mexican American Movement independent of the YMCA. Like the LULACs, MAM was seen as an elite rather than a mass organization. It emphasized the development of a leadership group of Chicano professionals, and its membership consisted of schoolteachers, social workers, lawyers, doctors, and managers (Munoz, 1981:30, 36).

In their definition of political goals and aspirations, the Mexican American Movement and the youth clubs sounded a great deal like OSA and LULAC. A 1941 platform noted, among other points:

The chief purpose of our Mexican Youth Conference, as young Americans of Mexican descent, is to better conditions among our Mexican race living in the United States and to serve constructively in the great nation we are privileged to live in.

Through a process of education we believe that our rising Mexican youth is continually reaching higher achievements and goals in regard to American standards of living (cited in Munoz, 1981:19).

The attitude of this organization toward its ethnic identity can best be described as one of ambivalence. On the one hand, statements from the *Mexican American Voice* often extolled the virtues of idealized Spanish and Aztec civilizations, and urged their readers to maintain their bilingualism and to hold on to the best of their heritage. At the same time, other statements blamed elements of that same heritage for holding Mexican Americans back. One issue of the *Mexican American Voice* states that

the beauty of this great democracy lies in the freedom of thought and expression which grants these people the privileges of thinking as they wish, but oftentimes we see these people working a great harm for themselves by passing up great opportunities for self-betterment because of a mistaken sense of loyalty to their cultural background (ibid., 21).

In the minds of the MAM leadership, it seems that ethnic pride was to function as a stepping-stone for upward mobility, and thus eventually, for full integration into U.S. society.

Despite the high hopes that its leadership had, the Mexican American Movement did not do well after the end of World War II. It did not attain its goals in terms of either funding or membership, and it had ceased to exist by the end of the decade. Nevertheless, many of its members went on to help establish other California-based organizations in the postwar period, including the Community Service Organization (CSO) and the Mexican American Political Association (MAPA) (ibid., 37, 40).

THE POSTWAR GROUPS: EMERGENCE OF A SERVICE ORIENTATION

World War II was a watershed for Chicano political and community organizations. Chicanos who fought in the war were to form a political generation. The standard interpretation is that Chicano veterans returned to society to find that the democratic ideals for which they had fought were not realized for their own people (Cuellar, 1969:16). Something like a revolution of rising expectations had taken place. It is also true that many of the employment opportunities that had opened up for Chicanos during the wartime labor shortage dried up after the war, and this may have been a contributing factor.

Two groups that were formed after the war in different parts of the Southwest illustrate the changed nature of Chicano organizations. The first of these was the American G.I. Forum, established in south Texas by Chicano veterans in 1948. The initial motivation for its formation had to do with the difficulties they had in securing the government benefits due them as veterans (Allsup, 1982:34–35). By the end of the year, the G.I. Forum had forty chapters in Texas (ibid., 36). Eventually, it became a national organization.

The G.I. Forum from the beginning was politically oriented, and although officially nonpartisan, it has remained close to the Democratic party. Members participated actively in the Viva Kennedy! clubs of 1960. Like the LULACs and OSA, it was concerned with issues of discrimination against Chicanos in a number of social areas, including school segregation, political representation, discrimination in the purchase of real estate, and civil rights in general (ibid., 38, 65). Not unexpectedly, given changing circumstances, it did not place the same heavy stress on assimilation as these other groups.

The most distinctive aspect of the G.I. Forum, however, was the combination of antidiscrimination activities with a service orientation. This orientation went beyond efforts to break down obstacles to full racial equality, and moved in the direction of the direct provision of services to Chicanos. Among these services are scholarships for Chicano college students, job training programs, and the construction of low-cost housing (Tirado, 1970:70).

Another important group that was formed in the same year, the Community Service Organization (CSO), illustrates the same trend. The CSO was organized originally in the Los Angeles area by a group that included a number of veterans. Its concern with social issues in the Chicano community led to its participation in electoral campaigns for Edward Roybal, including an unsuccessful 1947 bid for the Los Angeles City Council and a successful 1949 race for the same office. These campaigns involved the CSO with an organizer named Fred Ross, sent to California to organize Chicanos by Saul Alinsky's Industrial Areas Foundation. Ross assisted the Los Angeles CSO in mounting voter registration drives, which remained a CSO priority thereafter (Marin, 1980:60–62). Cesar Chavez, recruited to CSO in San Jose by Fred Ross in 1952, began his organizing career with voter registration drives (Levy, 1975:98–104).

The CSO did not restrict membership to citizens, nor did it require English as a condition for membership. In keeping with the strong Alinsky influence, it emphasized grass-roots organizing. Much of the leadership was middle class or white collar, although Chavez, who rose to be a director of the CSO, had been a migrant farm-worker. During the 1950s, the CSO continued its political work, although it moved to a nonpartisan stance. It focused on issues such as police brutality, educational reform, and integrated housing. Chavez and others were involved at this time in trying to end the bracero program (ibid., 129ff). The CSO also conducted a major campaign to secure state old-age pensions for noncitizens (Tirado, 1970:64). In the 1960s, it moved, as the G.I. Forum had, to a service orientation (Marin, 1980:68). Although it characterized this move as a return to a "mutual aid" approach, and even provided the traditional death-benefit insurance, it is clear that this was not a traditional mutual aid program. Among the services it provided were a credit union and a Buyers' Club and Consumer Complaint Center (Tirado, 1970:64). Chavez describes his own awareness of the utility of a service in the following passage:

Well, one night it just hit me. Once you helped people, most became very loyal. The people who helped us back when we wanted volunteers were the people we had helped. So I began to get a group of those people around me. Once I realized helping people was an organizing technique, I increased that work. I was willing to work day and night and go to hell and back for people—provided they also did something for CSO in return. . . . For a long time we didn't know how to put that work together into an organization. But we learned after a while. . . . I think solving problems for people is the only way to build solid groups (Levy, 1975:111).

While Chavez here depicts the service orientation in a strictly in-strumental manner, it took on a life of its own for the CSO and other organizations.

The Nature of a Service Orientation

These groups differ from preexisting Chicano organizations in directly providing services to the Chicano population. Typical ser-vices include the provision of housing, medical care, legal aid, job training, adult and other special education, career counseling, con-sumer advice, drug counseling, halfway houses, and so on. The direct provision of services shares with antidiscrimination activities the objective of reducing inequality or the effects of inequality in the society. For that reason, I believe that the two types of activities as practiced by Chicano organizations can be seen as related dimensions of one general goal.

The service orientation differs from the older mutual-aid approach in that the mutualistas depended entirely on their own resources to provide their particular benefits. Service oriented groups, on the other hand, typically rely on resources from the outside in the form of public funds, foundation or corporate contributions, or volunteer work.

Many Chicano organizations, such as the CSO and G.I. Forum, provided services as one component of an overall program that included several types of activities. In recent years, a number of ethnic organizations have come into existence for the sole and specific purpose of providing services. Such organizations include community health and legal clinics, community development corporations, and a variety of others. Toward the end of the 1950s and into the 1960s, a number of preexisting organizations that did not originally engage in the direct provision of services, such as the LULACs, tended to take on such an orientation (Fraga, 1980:46).

While a number of factors probably influenced this transformation, it is logical to assume that the decline over time of the more overt and blatant forms of racial discrimination made the provision of services a more salient issue. Certainly, the growth of the federal budget and the availability of funds through such programs as the War on Poverty and Model Cities served to spur the development of a service orientation in Chicano organizations.

EXPLICITLY POLITICAL GROUPS: MAPA AND PASSO

Toward the end of the period under consideration, Chicano organizations appeared that were finally explicitly political. The first, organized in California in 1959, made its orientation as unambiguous as possible by calling itself the Mexican American Political Association. This predominantly middle class group arose because of widespread dissatisfaction with Chicano influence in the California Democratic party in the 1950s, and after two frustrating defeats of

Chicano candidates for statewide office (Tirado, 1970:66; Burt, 1982a:3–4). While MAPA is not officially aligned with either major party, its relationship to the Democratic party historically has been very close. In recent years, however, there has been a significant influx of Republicans into the organization (Burt, 1982b:256ff). Not at all service oriented, MAPA has concentrated on voter registration, political education, lobbying, endorsing and recommending candidates, and on antidiscrimination activities around such historically popular issues as police malpractice and school problems (Tirado, 1970:67).

In 1960, a specifically political Chicano organization was formed in Texas, inspired in part by the Viva Kennedy! clubs and by the example of MAPA. This organization was named the Political Association of Spanish-Speaking Organizations (PASSO) (Guzman, 1966:380; Chandler, 1968:159; Cuellar, 1969:43). Shortly thereafter, delegates met in Arizona to form a Chicano umbrella political group with the same name. Delegates were present from such diverse groups as MAPA, LULAC, the CSO, the Alianza Hispano-Americana, and the G.I. Forum. The organization never reached its intended national scope, however, and has been active primarily in Texas, where its orientation is similar to MAPA's (Guzman, 1966:381).

CONCLUSION

In the period from 1920 to 1960, a number of groups emerged whose primary political goal was equality. Various activities were undertaken by these groups in pursuit of that goal, including lobbying, lawsuits, publicity, voter registration, political endorsements, the provision of services, and general organizing. Whatever the approach, the common goal was the reduction of racial inequality by bringing down the barriers to upward mobility for Chicanos. The approach, then, was essentially an integrationist one, in that it attempted to increase Chicano representation in the schools, the labor unions, the corporations, the government, and the other major institutions.

4

The Chicano Movement
and the Revival of
Community

The decade of the 1960s was a turbulent period during which there emerged a complex interaction between Chicano organizations and political trends in the society at large. The result was an explosion of political activity and new political organizations in the second half of the decade, extending into the 1970s. This development, without parallel in Chicano history, is referred to as the Chicano Movement and represents a third stage in the evolution of Chicano ethnic goals. Movement organizations incorporated much that had gone before, while adding distinctive new elements.

ANTECEDENTS: POLITICAL TRENDS

A number of changes were taking place in United States politics that had important repercussions for Chicanos. The presidential election year of 1960 saw a new, more progressive administration in Washington, giving rise to a different set of expectations. Many old and new Chicano political activists had participated in the Viva Kennedy! clubs, resulting in a new impetus for organizational activity, which was expressed in groups like PASSO. Kennedy's youthful liberalism and Catholic affiliation attracted Chicano political enthusiasm as no other recent presidential candidate had.

The civil rights movement had been picking up steam during the 1950s, and the political changes in Washington reinforced its energy. In time, civil rights came to be seen as an issue affecting Chicanos as well as blacks. These political trends resulted in affirmative action programs in colleges and universities and helped create a small but growing number of Chicano college students. They were to become an important political factor in the 1960s.

Particularly after 1964, the Kennedy-Johnson administrations instituted such new government programs as the War on Poverty, which had both a direct and indirect impact on Chicano communities. In addition to providing resources around which community politics could be mobilized, these programs produced political activists from the ranks of their staffs. Rodolfo Corky Gonzales, to cite one example, had been a director of a War on Poverty program in Denver before becoming one of the leading Chicano political movers of the decade.

The year 1964 also saw the birth of the Free Speech movement on the Berkeley campus, the kickoff for the student movement that was to convulse college campuses for years. Ferment on the campus acted as a further stimulant to Chicano student activism, which in turn fed into numerous off-campus political organizations.

ANTECEDENTS: CHICANO ORGANIZATIONS

In a sense, all of the Chicano organizations that had gone before were antecedents to the Chicano Movement, since they had maintained an unbroken tradition of struggle and a process of recruitment of new activists. In some cases, we can see the effects particularly clearly. PASSO, for example, was involved in 1963 in the takeover of the Crystal City, Texas, city council by a group of insurgent local Chicanos. While that takeover was of short duration, it involved a then nineteen-year-old student, José Angel Gutierrez, who was to return to his hometown in 1969 to lead a second and more profound Chicano revolt that was the founding event of La Raza Unida party (Shockley, 1974:37). In a similar manner, the activities of the Mexican American Movement contributed to the emergence of organizations such as the CSO.

The formation of the United Farm Workers (UFW) in 1962 was also an important precursor of later "movement" organizations. Although the UFW is a labor organization rather than a political or community group, its predominantly Chicano membership, its aura of moral crusade, and the self-conscious use of Mexican symbolism attracted many nonworker followers, including many students, to "La Causa." Its innovative tactics and the visibility of its low-key charismatic leader also aided immeasurably in projecting Chicanos onto the national political scene. The success of the UFW was due in part, of course, to the organizational skills that Cesar Chavez had gained as an organizer for CSO.

Another Chicano organization that came into existence in the first half of the 1960s was in some ways an anomaly, but it nevertheless exercised a strong influence on the future course of the Chicano Movement. This was the Alianza Federal de Mercedes, later known as the Alianza Federal de Pueblos Libres, founded by Reies Tijerina in northern New Mexico in 1963. In its papers of incorporation, the Alianza states its purpose:

To organize and acquaint the Heirs of all the Spanish Land Grants covered by the Guadalupe Hidalgo Treaty . . . [t]hus providing unity of purpose and securing for the Heirs of Spanish Land Grants the highest advantages as provided by the afore-said Treaty and Constitutions (of the United States and State of Mexico) (Gardner, 1970:96).

Since the days of Las Gorras Blancas, the residents of northern New Mexico villages have carried on a struggle to reclaim their lost lands and to hold on to what remains. In this process, they have formed land grant corporations, engaged in extended lawsuits, emulated Las Gorras Blancas' direct-action tactics on a smaller scale, and engaged in electoral politics. None of these tactics proved effective in the long run, as the land reconcentrated in the hands of large Anglo ranchers and corporations and the U.S. Forest Service, and the villages continued their decline. Part of the anomaly of the Alianza is that it faithfully echoed the nineteenth-century struggle that had been forgotten elsewhere.

Another part of the anomaly resided in its electrifying leader, an outsider (from Texas) in a land of ingrown villages and families, a Protestant preacher in an overwhelmingly Catholic area, a man given to intense mystical visions and spellbinding oratory. Tijerina was the only leader in the twentieth century who had been able to bring together representatives from different land grants into a single organization to press their claims (Swadesh, 1968:166). His in-

ability to form a solid organization was the Achilles' heel of the
Alianza, however, as shown by its rapid decline after Tijerina's jail-
ing in 1969. The Alianza was the only major Chicano political organization to have been founded in New Mexico in this century—
most of the others had their base in either Texas or California.
Eventually, Tijerina became a national figure, and toward the
latter part of the 1960s, was attempting to broaden the ideological
base of the Alianza to include civil rights issues, and also was ex-
ploring alliances with blacks, Native Americans, and other groups
(Gardner, 1970; Chapter 16). The hard core of his followers in
northern New Mexico, however, apparently preferred to maintain
a narrow focus on the grants (Herz, 1971; Herz, 1970:688, 848).
Thus, I believe it is correct to say that the Alianza was much like
the Chicano organizations of the early twentieth century, with a
more or less exclusive focus on matters directly related to community cohesion. This "communitarian" interpretation is partially
borne out by Frances Swadesh, who reports on the effects of one
of the Alianza's tactics, that of occupying and living temporarily on
National Forest lands that had been taken from the community
land grants:

The experience of living together under the community legal code and
customary rules of their ancestors, often wistfully recollected by their
grandparents, revived among Alianza members a sense of the vitality of
their traditional value system. The feeling for solidary [sic] relations of the
community, reaching beyond the ties of the extended kin group, was expressed by many Alianza members after the San Joaquin [community land
grant] experience, and has become crystallized in strong ties of loyalty and
affection among the members (Swadesh, 1968:171).

EL PLAN ESPIRITUAL DE AZTLAN

The pace of Chicano political activism picked up in 1967, with
the formation of the Brown Berets in California and MAYO (Mexican American Youth Organization) in Texas. The Berets were a
paramilitary organization aimed at barrio youth and gang members, while MAYO was one of a number of student groups that
were being formed around this same period. In 1968, a series of
dramatic school walkouts by Chicano high school students oc-

curred in Los Angeles, and in 1969, the first national Chicano Youth Liberation Conference took place in Denver. All of these events demonstrated the growing involvement of young Chicanos in political activity.

The 1969 Chicano Youth Conference, organized by Corky Gonzales and his Denver-based Crusade for Justice, attracted hundreds of participants from throughout the Southwest. It was at this conference that Gonzales unveiled El Plan Espiritual de Aztlan, a statement that both documented and further stimulated the wave of Chicano nationalism that was then sweeping the Southwest. Borrowing the concept of Aztlan from Aztec references to their ancestral homeland, the plan reads in part:

In the spirit of a new people that is conscious not only of the proud historical heritage but also of the brutal "gringo" invasion of our territories, we, the Chicano inhabitants and civilizers of the northern land of Aztlan from whence came our forefathers, reclaiming the land of their birth and consecrating the determination of our people of the sun, declare that the call of our blood is our power, our responsibility, and our inevitable destiny . . .

Brotherhood unites us, and love for our brothers makes us a people whose time has come and who struggles against the foreigner "gabacho" who exploits our riches and destroys our culture. With our heart in our hands and our hands in the soil, we declare the independence of our mestizo nation. We are a bronze people with a bronze culture. Before the world, before all of North America, before all our brothers in the bronze continent, we are a nation, we are a union of free pueblos, we are Aztlan. Por La Raza todo, Fuera de La Raza nada.

PROGRAM

El Plan Espiritual de Aztlan sets the theme that the Chicanos (La Raza de Bronze) must use their nationalism as the key or common denominator for mass mobilization and organization. Once we are committed to the idea and philosophy of El Plan de Aztlan, we can only conclude that social, economic, cultural, and political independence is the only road to total liberation from oppression, exploitation, and racism. Our struggle then must be for the control of our barrios, campos, pueblos, lands, our economy, our culture, and our political life. El Plan commits all levels of Chicano society—the barrio, the campo, the ranchero, the writer, the teacher, the worker, the professional—to La Causa.

NATIONALISM

Nationalism as the key of organization transcends all religious, political, class, and economic factions or boundaries. Nationalism is the common denominator that all members of La Raza can agree upon.

ORGANIZATIONAL GOALS

Economy: economic control of our lives and our communities can only come about by driving the exploiter out of our communities, our pueblos, and our lands and by controlling and developing our own talents, sweat and resources. . . . Lands rightfully ours will be acquired by the community for the people's welfare. . . .

Education must be relative to our people, i.e., history, culture, bilingual education, contributions, etc. Community control of our schools, our teachers, our administrators, our counselors, and our programs. . . . Cultural values of our people strengthen our identity and the moral backbone of the movement. Our culture unites and educates the family of La Raza towards liberation with our heart and mind. We must insure that our writers, poets, musicians, and artists produce literature and art that is appealing to our people and relates to our revolutionary culture. Our cultural values of life, family, and home will serve as a powerful weapon to defeat that gringo dollar value system and encourage the process of love and brotherhood.

Political liberation can come only through independent action on our part, since the two-party system is the same animal with two heads that feed from the same trough. . . .

ACTION

. . . Creation of an independent local, regional, and national political party. A nation autonomous and free—culturally, socially, economically, and politically—will make its own decisions on the usage of our lands, the taxation of our goods, the utilization of our bodies for war, the determination of justice (reward and punishment), and the profit of our sweat.

El Plan de Aztlan is the plan of liberation! (*Documents of the Chicano Struggle*, 1971:4–6).

There are several notable aspects of the Plan de Aztlan. One is the deliberate reference to the Indian part of the Chicano heritage, a striking departure from traditional Chicano political statements. Another is the very strong focus on culture and the preservation of the Chicano cultural heritage, a focus that led this ideological thrust to being labeled cultural nationalism. The call for an independent Chicano party is also significant, anticipating the creation of La Raza Unida party in Texas shortly thereafter.

One of the more distinctive features of the plan was that it tied together a strong communitarian orientation with an equally strong commitment to equality and antidiscrimination. For the first time in a major programmatic statement, community identity and ethnic equality had been not only raised simultaneously but intimately linked. While the plan did not really make explicit whether it was calling for secession from the United States, it was very clear that it foresaw no possibility of ending oppression without Chicano control of the institutions that directly affected community life. This was very different from the preceding generation's emphasis on achieving equality through gaining access to the dominant institutions of the society, and thus becoming integrated into those institutions.

It is no coincidence that the Plan de Aztlan was launched at a youth conference, since Corky Gonzales was seen by Chicano youth as their ideological leader (Acuña, 1981:364). The plan had a special impact on those students and other Chicanos who had been brought up in the cities of the Southwest in the postwar era. It spoke of the value of Chicano and Mexicano culture to students who had grown up in a society that let them know in a thousand subtle and not so subtle ways that their culture was inferior. It stressed community and the solidarity of all Chicanos to a group that had been raised in an urban, acculturative milieu that often left profound doubts about that group's own cultural identity and created gaps between the generations. College students in particular felt cut off from their communities on campuses they experienced as alien institutions, far removed from the barrios, and where they were a small minority.

Gonzales was himself a product of such an upbringing, and he was able in the Plan de Aztlan and in his epic poem, *I Am Joaquin,* to couch his political and cultural appeals in a way that produced an instant response from an entire generation of Chicano youth. The themes of the Plan de Aztlan spread far and wide after the Denver Youth conferences.

LA RAZA UNIDA PARTY

The political activism of the 1960s culminated in the formation of La Raza Unida party in 1969–1970. It began in Crystal City, Texas, as an outgrowth of a project conceived by the student or-

ganization MAYO (Shockley, 1974:114ff; I. Garcia, 1987). Jose Angel Gutierrez, a member of MAYO, returned to his hometown with
the intention of developing a strategy for the community control of
local institutions, and ended up as the founder of the party. The
success of the party in gaining control of the city council and later
the board of education in this predominantly Chicano south Texas
town gained the party instant fame and led to the formation of
Raza Unida chapters elsewhere. By 1970, it had spread to Colorado, and in California, chapters were started throughout the state.

La Raza Unida's greatest successes were in south Texas, although there were other successes in local races in widely scattered locales. The effort to make it a viable statewide organization,
however, failed in each of the southwestern states. The high point
of the party came in 1972, when a national convention in El Paso
drew hundreds of delegates and the active participation of Gutierrez, Corky Gonzales, and Reies Tijerina. After 1972, the party declined rapidly in California and more slowly in its original Texas
strongholds.

A notable feature of the party was the active role of students and
other youth. In California, the majority of the chapters depended
heavily on students for both leaders and rank-and-file members
(Munoz and Barrera, 1982). In Texas, the party grew out of a student organization, although later it broadened its base of support,
in areas like Crystal City, to include the Chicano working class.

The goal orientation of the party was strongly nationalistic, as
was true of the Plan de Aztlan, and this led very naturally to an
emphasis on the community control of institutions. The closely related themes of antiassimilation and self-determination were also
interwoven into most party programmatic statements and speeches
by its leaders. At the same time, party activists were also strongly
committed to specific issues involving discriminatory practices. Some
representative quotes illustrate the party's goal orientation and show
how these themes were integrally connected:

RAZA UNIDA PARTY PREAMBLE (Texas statewide platform)

La Raza, recognizing the need to replace the existing system with a hu-
manistic alternative which shall maintain equal representation of all people;

And, recognizing the need to create a government which serves the needs of individual communities, yet is beneficial to the general populace;

And, recognizing the need to create a political movement dedicated to ending the causes of poverty, misery and injustice so that future generations can live a life free from exploitation;

And, recognizing the need to abolish racist practices within the existing social, educational, economic and political system so that physical and cultural genocidal practices against minorities will be discontinued;

Therefore resolve, to these ends, because we are the people who have been made aware of the needs of the many through our suffering, who have learned the significance of carnalismo, the strength of *la familia* and the importance of people working together; and recognizing the natural right of all peoples to preserve their self-identity and to formulate their own destiny,

To Establish Raza Unida Party, with courage and love in our hearts, a firm commitment to mankind, and with peace in our minds (*Texas Raza Unida Party*, n.d.).

The state party platform goes on to list a number of suggested reforms in the areas of education, the political system, taxation and economic policies, the court and prison systems, the status of women, immigration, military service, natural resources, health, welfare, and housing.

EL PLAN DE SANTA BARBARA AND THE CONSOLIDATION OF MECHA

After La Raza Unida, the other prototypical Chicano "movement" organizations were the student groups and the emerging Chicano Studies programs at colleges and universities. Much of the ideology of these organizations is reflected in a document entitled El Plan de Santa Barbara (Chicano Coordinating Council on Higher Education, 1969).

This plan was the result of a statewide conference held at Santa Barbara, California, in April, 1969. The conference and the resulting plan were in many ways an attempt to elaborate on the themes and goals raised at the earlier Denver Youth Conference and in the Plan Espiritual de Aztlan. The aim was to apply these goals in a concrete manner to the college campuses by developing a master plan for Chicano higher education, including the development of a unified Chicano student movement (Munoz, 1981:59–65).

The strong communitarian and antiassimilation orientation of the plan is expressed throughout.

> For decades Mexican people in the United States struggled to realize the "American Dream." And some—a few—have. But the cost, the ultimate cost of assimilation, required turning away from el barrio and la colonia. . . .
>
> . . . the self-determination of our community is now the only acceptable mandate for social and political action; it is the essence of Chicano commitment. . . . [T]he widespread use of the term Chicano today signals a rebirth of pride and confidence. Chicanismo simply embodies an ancient truth: that man is never closer to his true self as when he is close to his community.
>
> Chicanismo involves a crucial distinction in political consciousness between a Mexican American and a Chicano mentality. The Mexican American is a person who lacks respect for his cultural and ethnic heritage. Unsure of himself, he seeks assimilation as a way out of his "degraded" social status. . . . In contrast, Chicanismo reflects self-respect and pride in one's ethnic and cultural background. . . . Mexican Americans must be viewed as potential Chicanos. . . . Cultural nationalism is a means of total Chicano liberation (ibid., 9, 50–51).

El Plan de Santa Barbara called for the creation of Chicano Studies programs and discussed the nature of their curriculums, stressing the reinforcement of cultural heritage and the formation of a sense of community (ibid., 40).

According to the analysis of the plan, the institutions of higher learning in the United States are controlled by and serve the interests of the wealthy and powerful. Yet these were the same institutions to which Chicanos were now trying to gain greater access. Might not the success of these efforts lead to co-optation on a massive scale? There was some attempt to wrestle with the implications of this dilemma in the plan, even if only in a very partial and incomplete manner.

> Traditionally, the goals of higher education have been directed to meet the demands of the ruling strata of society by training the specialized man-

power required for the operation of their demands. The equivalent practice today is found in training students in higher education to serve corporate industry and public agencies: the two major economic entities of
society. The socialization and indoctrination of these "students" to conform to this function and accept this limited range of alternatives is a
corollary role of higher education today. Once properly trained, these students serve as agents of the controlling powers and in turn serve to perpetuate this process. . . . Therefore all attempts to project Chicanos into
the mainstream of higher education as it exists today are equivalent to
enslaving La Raza to the controlling powers of this society. . . .
    Rather than accommodate Chicanos to these institutions, support pro-
grams should facilitate the development of educational processes to meet
the unique interests of Chicanos . . . [and to] develop alternative goals
to those prescribed by society. . . . It cannot be overemphasized that the
focus of Chicano efforts on campus must provide "new" meaning and value
to higher learning. Chicano programs must not employ existing goals and
structures of higher education as a frame of reference. To succumb to
traditional structures and approaches is to legitimize their role in indoc-
trinating Chicanos to become a part of gabacho [a pejorative term for Anglo—MB] society (Munoz, 1981:30).

Exactly how a small and newly arrived campus minority was to
accomplish this massive task was left unresolved by the plan.
    Despite ambiguities, the plan achieved a great deal of success in
the short run. After its publication, a large number of Chicano
Studies programs were in fact instituted in colleges and universities, particularly in California but also in other southwestern and
some midwestern states. The plan had also called for the consolidation of various embryonic Chicano student organizations, and this
was largely accomplished also. The unified student organization
became known by the acronym MECHA, which stood for Movi-
miento Estudiantil Chicano de Aztlan (Chicano Student Movement
of Aztlan). Since the word "mecha" is also slang for "match," the
term was intended to convey a feeling of militance and a concept
of the organization as a spark for political action. This student group
was to play a vital role in the next few years in mobilizing La Raza
Unida and other organizations, following through on the Plan de
Santa Barbara's call for the integration of campus and community
action.

CONCLUSION

The Chicano Movement of the 1960s and '70s drew on the heritage of Chicano political activism but added distinctive new elements, such as the heavy involvement of youth and the emphasis on academic programs. However, the most distinctive element was the combining of communitarian and egalitarian goals under the ideological label of Chicanismo, and what might be seen as an almost nostalgic vision of community.

Although this period saw the publication of various "plans" and other political statements, a great deal of ambiguity remained. The exact ways in which the two major goals were to be combined and implemented were never spelled out, so that it was difficult to translate the goals into a concrete course of action. As a result, it became possible in the subsequent period for political groups to go off in very different directions, while still claiming to remain faithful to the goals of the movement.

The vagueness of the ideology also made it difficult for activists to recognize the potential contradictions in what they were trying to accomplish, a topic discussed in Part II of this book.

5

Postmovement Trends: Fragmentation, Radicalization, Retraditionalization

INTRODUCTION

The "classic" phase of the Chicano movement was marked by El Plan Espiritual de Aztlan, the Crusade for Justice, La Raza Unida party, El Plan de Santa Barbara, and the formation of MECHA, with the peak years of activity being 1968 to 1973. These various plans and organizations (along with a number of others of lesser importance) mutually reinforced each other, and their most distinctive feature was the blending of communitarian and egalitarian ideals. With the decline of the Chicano Movement, a number of complex and often conflicting trends set in, among them ideological fragmentation, a dilution of the communitarian emphasis, and a resurgence of traditional Chicano organizations. These trends can be illustrated through an examination of several Chicano organizations of the 1970s and '80s: CASA, the ATM, the National Council of La Raza, Communities Organized for Public Service (COPS), and the United Neighborhoods Organization (UNO).

THE RISE AND DECLINE OF RADICAL SECTARIANISM: CASA and ATM

Radical political ideologies locate the source of social problems in the very structure of a particular society, in the ways in which that society is organized at a basic level. As a result, they advocate major changes, even revolutionary changes, in that structure as a means of solving those problems. This type of analysis has been applied to poverty, racism, war, imperialism, environmental destruction, patriarchy, and other social issues. During the height of the Chicano Movement, there were no Chicano political organizations that could be called radical in this sense, although there were radical individuals and groups within the major organizations.

Paralleling developments in other U.S. political movements of the times, radical ideologies began to have more impact on Chicanos in the early 1970s. These changes often began in the existing organizations but eventually resulted in the formation of new, explicitly radical groups. These new organizations were guided by one variety or another of Marxist ideology, although with a distinctly Chicano flavor.

Within MECHA, for example, Marxists began to criticize the dominant ideology of cultural nationalism. A statewide MECHA conference at Riverside, California, in 1973 resulted in a major split and a walkout by the Marxist faction (Munoz, 1981:71–72).

Within La Raza Unida party, there was also ideological ferment, although only one chapter, the Los Angeles-based Labor Committee, was predominantly Marxist. Many of the more radicalized members of the Partido eventually left to join Marxist organizations (Munoz and Barrera, 1982:114–15). The Labor Committee later became the nucleus of the August Twenty-Ninth Movement (ATM), discussed below.

CASA

The most important radical Chicano organization to emerge during this period was CASA (Centro de Accion Social Autonomo, or Center for Autonomous Social Action). This organization was primarily responsible in the 1970s for focusing attention on the immigration issue and for redefining the dominant Chicano attitude toward undocumented workers from Mexico (Garcia, 1985:217–20). Traditionally, Chicano political organizations had seen the presence of undocumented workers (and contract workers from Mexico) as detrimental to the interests of Mexican Americans, particularly in undercutting efforts to organize Chicano workers into unions. The American G.I. Forum, for instance, called, in the 1950s, for stricter enforcement of immigration laws and supported the federal government's infamous 1954 "Operation Wetback" (Allsup, 1982:105, 108–9, 114, 126). The United Farm Workers Union during its early history was also active in campaigning against the presence of undocumented workers, whom the growers used to break strikes and put pressure on wages.

The history of CASA can be divided into two distinct phases, the first moderate and the second radical. The organization began in 1968 as a spin-off of MAPA. One of its chief organizers was past MAPA president Bert Corona, a longtime labor organizer. From the start, CASA committed itself to support of the trade union struggle and especially to the defense of the undocumented worker (Gutierrez, 1982:8–10). In addition to such activities as strike support, the organization involved itself in the direct provision of social services for the undocumented. With this approach, CASA rapidly built up its membership and opened centers in several major southwestern and midwestern cities. According to its financial records, it could count on 5,000 dues-paying members in the Los Angeles area alone in 1972 (ibid., 22). The structure of the organization remained very decentralized.

In 1974, however, CASA entered into a more overtly ideological and more radical phase. This change was linked to the influx into CASA of a new group of activists drawn from the ranks of students, professionals, and community organizers (*History of CASA*: 12–15).[1] Some members of this new cadre came from the Comite Estudiantil del Pueblo, a Marxist group made up of Chicano students who were dissatisfied with MECHA's political ideology (Munoz, 1981:73–75). The bulk of these new CASA activists, however, came from an organization named the National Committee to Free Los Tres (CFLT). The CFLT, which had initially been formed to defend three young Chicano antidrug activists in Los Angeles from criminal charges, was controlled by a collective of thirty-five organized around the study of Marxism-Leninism (*History of CASA*: 19–20).

Some of the flavor of the CFLT ideology, which counterposed "revolutionary nationalism" to "cultural nationalism," can be gathered from the following:

. . . some Chicano Movement activists obsessively continue to hold on to the view that we must struggle against exploitation, racism, repression and

for self determination, guided by the spiritual, cultural and moral values
of our Indian ancestors. . . . [They] . . . also hold the view that since
the white European Invader is our oppressor, we must reject any ideas
. . . that come from white people. . . . But the problems our people
face today . . . require concrete solutions . . . Cultural practices, spiritual beliefs, love . . . Chicanismo . . . do not teach us how to organize a
workers strike, how to organize the struggle against police brutality, how
to stop the dragnet raids and mass deportations of our people, how to
organize a student movement. . . . It does not teach us how to create a
society free of exploitation, how as part of the working class we can take
power. . . . Our children should not feel proud that they are Mexicanos
only because of their color. The strongest national consciousness comes
from a knowledge that the masses of our people have made great contributions to the progress and development of organized society, industry
and agriculture . . . led . . . great struggles to organize workers against
exploitation. . . . Teaching history in this manner . . . creates strong
pride in our heritage. But it also recognizes and respects the role of other
nationalities as workers and . . . teaches our people true internationalism.
It exposes the class nature of US society . . . imperialism as the bloodiest,
most brutal exploiter . . . responsible for the underdevelopment of the
Third World. . . . [We] . . . also learn the true nature of racism as having an economic base. . . . [R]evolutionary nationalism entails working
class solidarity which knows no borders. A concept especially important
to us who exist divided from our people by the border established by the
imperialist US powers. True revolutionary nationalism can only be developed in this context. Un people sin fronteras (*Sin Cadenas*, as quoted in
Munoz, 1981:74–75).

This represented quite an ideological distance from El Plan Espiritual de Aztlan, articulated only five years earlier! This statement also anticipates much of the later ideology of CASA; indeed,
the CASA paper established by radical activists came to bear the
name *Sin Fronteras* (No Borders).

As the CFLT cadre moved into CASA in bulk in 1974, they
transformed the internal dynamics of that organization. The established leadership, of whom Bert Corona was the best known member, continued to emphasize the organization of and direct provision of services to undocumented and other workers, and
participation in reform-oriented electoral politics (Gutierrez,
1982:12). The new group preferred to focus on radical political education and wanted to take on a much broader range of issues,

domestic and international, while deemphasizing the service orientation. The ensuing conflict resulted in the departure of Corona and the old-line leadership in 1974. In 1975, three chapters of CASA in different cities also withdrew from the organization over the new ideological thrust (ibid., 15). The new direction was signaled in six principles that came out of a 1975 national CASA conference:

(1) Uphold Marxism-Leninism as the basic ideology of CASA (2) Work around a strategy with the principle objective of building national unity of the Mexican people (3) The principle force to build national unity of the Mexican people were Mexican workers who should be mobilized into the class struggle by promoting their participation in the trade unionist movement and in the struggle of Mexican people for full equality and democratic rights (4) The Organization should be of one nationality, Mexican (5) It's [sic] structure would include three levels of membership [,] one of which, the base membership, would not be subject to the same discipline as the other two levels, which would adhere to democratic centralism in order to ensure that CASA would be both selective and massive, and (6) *Sin Fronteras* was to begin publication immediately out of Los Angeles [in] 1975 (*History of CASA*:25–26).

Once begun, the process of ideological struggle was not easy to contain. In 1977, there was another split with the departure of Carlos Vasquez, one of CASA's key ideologists and a prime mover behind *Sin Fronteras*, followed a few months later by 80 percent of the paper's staff (ibid., 36–37, 55).

Some of the ideological questions that continued to bedevil the organization were listed in an internal document:

Is the struggle of the Mexican people in the United States a National Movement to retake the territories of the Southwest annexed by the United States in the war of 1846? What is the relationship in the role of the Mexican Peoples movement in the United States to the general class struggle for socialism in the United States?

Is the building of a Leninist party-type organization of the Mexican people in the United States, that is, one nationality, politically and ideologically correct in a multi-national society? Or to put it in other words, was CASA dividing the working class movement in the United States?

Questions with regards to strategy such as is the strategic objective of building national unity of the Mexican people a measurable and correct objective? When we speak of building national unity, were we speaking of building national unity of the Mexican people in the United States or on both sides of the border? And considering the answer to this last question, should we be organizing CASA on both sides of the border?

In terms of short and long range work, questions developed such as how much emphasis should we concentrate on trade union work or popular work? And additionally, how much should we concentrate on the building of revolutionary organizations in the factories as opposed to the community or the universities?

Alarmed by the almost total absence of industrial workers within the membership some members questioned the class content of the Organization and asked for an answer to the question of how to emphasis [sic] work and recruitment amongst Mexican workers as opposed to professionals, students and community activists? (ibid., 31–32).

Given the "almost total absence of industrial workers within the membership" by 1977, answers to the other questions became moot. Total national membership had fallen below 1,000 by that time (Gutierrez, 1982:22), indicating that the new leadership had succeeded in three short years in decimating what had been a going organization. By 1978, it had for all practical purposes ceased to exist. In all fairness to CASA's young leadership, it should be kept in mind that many other organizations with roots in 1960s' activism withered on the vine in the 1970s.

The August Twenty-Ninth Movement

The other radical Chicano organization to appear in the 1970s was the August Twenty-Ninth Movement (ATM). Its original nucleus was in the Labor Committee of California's La Raza Unida party, a chapter that had steadily moved in a Marxist-Leninist direction. The ATM's activists sought to create a multinational (not just Chicano) Communist party that could take the vanguard role in educating and organizing U.S. workers to carry on a revolutionary struggle. However, it did not begin with an existing organization and a ready-made base as CASA did, and it never achieved a significant numerical following. While it never created a truly viable organization, then neither did it have the opportunity to destroy one.

The ATM shared with CASA an ideology that combined Marxist-Leninist and nationalist appeals, but in a very different fashion.

The ATM attempted to pattern itself on the teachings of Mao Tse-tung and their implementation in the People's Republic of China, whereas CASA was more oriented to the Soviet Union. The ATM also had a more strident and rhetorical tone than did CASA. Its most distinctive ideological element, however, was in its approach to the specific problems of Chicanos as a subordinate group in the United States. The ATM based its position on certain concepts Lenin and Stalin had developed to deal with the political problem of multiple ethnic groups in Russia and Eastern Europe before and after the Russian Revolution. The key concept here was that of national self-determination, which meant that any group that met certain criteria of "nationhood" was free to determine its own national boundaries, even if that meant seceding from an existing state. In its ideological pamphlet *Fan the Flames*, published around 1976, the ATM presented the results of its historical investigation into the situation of the Chicano people. The conclusion was that Chicanos did indeed fall within the established criteria, and were entitled to the right to secede as a guarantee against being oppressed by other ethnic groups. The ATM did not advocate that Chicanos in fact secede from the United States, only that they should have the right to do so and to establish their own state in their area of population concentration if they chose to do so by some unspecified mechanism.

In setting forth this position, the ATM distanced itself from the CASA ideology, which played down the distinction between Mexican and Chicano, stressing their common "Mexicanness" and the need to wage a struggle "sin fronteras" (ibid., 14–15, 17). While CASA ideologists attacked the concept of "Aztlan" as divisive, the ATM elevated it to a national principle.

The significance of the ATM, however, remained at the ideological level. Eventually, it merged with several other small Marxist-Leninist groups to form the League for Revolutionary Struggle, in effect abandoning its original ethnic identity.

The Impact of Radicalism

Virtually all radical organizations that operate in the Southwest have attempted to recruit Chicanos in a systematic way, but CASA and the ATM have been the only explicitly radical groups whose membership consisted primarily of Chicanos.[2] Even though neither remained in existence long, they did broaden the terms of the political debate, as well as raised the vital issue of the relation between the subordination of Chicanos and the capitalist structure of the American political economy.

In drawing on the Marxist tradition for their ideological concepts, these organizations took a very different position from other Chicano groups in the definition of goals. The goal of equality was traditionally dealt with by Chicanos only in terms of equality between the races. Shifting the debate to Marxist grounds added the themes of class inequality, inequality between men and women, and inequality between rich and poor countries. In addition, it added an intellectual dimension by linking these various types of inequality to each other through their common roots in the actions and interests of the dominant class in the United States.

Both organizations also redefined the communitarian ideal. CASA, although never resolving the issue to its own or others' satisfaction, argued that a focus on Chicanos apart from Mexicanos was too narrow. The ATM, on the other hand, made the international working class the focus of its allegiance and considered organizing on an ethnic, or "national," base to be primarily a tactical maneuver.

Limitations of the Sectarian Style

Whatever their innovations in the Chicano ideological arena, the impact of both CASA and the ATM was sharply limited by their styles of thinking and working. Both stand as classic examples of sectarian Marxism-Leninism, although the ATM was a purer case. There are several characteristics of this style, manifested not only by the ATM and CASA but all of the other self-designated Marxist-Leninist organizations that have operated in the barrios in recent years. Among these characteristics are the following:

(1) a predilection for slogans and formulas, with plenty of exclamation points and capitalized words. This is related to the quest for the "correct line," the set of formulas that will allow a group to function effectively as the vanguard of the revolution. Thus, in their 1974 Unity Statement, the ideologists of the ATM write:

Down with DOGMATISM and SECTARIANISM
Down with REVISIONISM
SUPPORT THE LIBERATION STRUGGLES OF ALL OPPRESSED
    NATIONALITIES
BUILD A GENUINE MULTI-NATIONAL COMMUNIST PARTY
WORKERS AND OPPRESSED PEOPLES OF THE WORLD UNITE
VENCEREMOS! (August Twenty-Ninth Movement, 1974:6).

In what must be a form of projection, these groups invariably accuse other left organizations of sectarianism.

(2) reliance on an orthodox, "official" terminology, perceived by outsiders as jargon and by insiders as a scientific vocabulary. Thus:

[A guiding principle is] [t]hat we correctly analyze and keep in mind the left deviation on the Chicano National Question of great nation and white chauvinism, and historically, the liquidation of the national question within the Southwest region by both the Trotskyites and the revisionist CPUSA. We must also be conscious in our investigation of this question of the right deviation of narrow nationalism and the overemphasizing of national characteristics to the detriment of proletarian internationalism (ibid., 5).

(3) the presence in the organization of an external line—the one put out for popular consumption and recruitment of the uninitiated—and an internal line—that which reflects the true thinking of the group's ideologists at the time. The external line is pushed by "front" groups, which are covertly controlled by a cadre of the core organization and which build their activities around one or more "legitimate" reform activities. Generally, although not always, the presence of the behind-the-scenes controlling group is known to all actors in the political arena, not to mention the FBI.

(4) overreliance on a process of argumentation based on the citing of a certain body of sacred texts, such as the *Collected Works* of Lenin or the writings of Mao or Stalin's *Principles of Leninism*, in order to bolster one's point of view.

(5) the mechanical application of "lessons" from successful revolutionary movements in other countries, such as Cuba, Vietnam, China, or the Soviet Union, without fully taking into account the very diffferent contexts in which those movements took place.

(6) an unwavering allegiance to one particular socialist country. Usually this is either the Soviet Union or China, although one Marxist-Leninist group finds the true source of inspiration in Albania. When a suitable

country does not exist, the object of allegiance may be a particular foreign ideologist, such as Trotsky or Mao.

(7) the structuring of the organization along the lines of "democratic centralism," modeled on the Bolshevik party led by Lenin. In essence, this amounts to democracy in theory and centralization in practice.

(8) a propensity for Left-group infighting, to the point that one sometimes gets the impression that other Left groups are seen as more of a threat than the capitalist class or the bourgeois state.

The complete and most developed form of the right deviation on Party building is to be found in the political line of the Revolutionary Union. These new revisionists are hostile to the science of Marxism-Leninism, only pay lip-service to it while they systematically attempt to wreck, slander or destroy any attempt by honest Marxist-Leninists to bring socialist consciousness to the working class. To do this at a time when the working class is under economic and political attack, when the spectre of advancing fascism sweeps the land, is to be nothing less than agents of imperialism and traitors to the working class (ibid., 14).

CASA and the ATM often engaged in this type of infighting with each other, and both hated the Trotskyist Socialist Workers Party (SWP), which was also trying to become the vanguard of the Chicano working class. CASA and the ATM carried on a bitter fight for control of the Chicano Studies program at California State University, Los Angeles; and CASA and the SWP's maneuvering wrecked the National Chicano/Latino Conference on Immigration held in San Antonio in 1977.

CASA was not quite as dogmatic and rigid as the ATM, and the rapid decline in its popular base after the radical takeover in 1974 led to considerable soul-searching and self-criticism, as noted above. Still, it did not occur to the remaining leadership to question whether there might not be deeper roots to the organization's problems, and whether the limitations it was encountering might not be inherent in the whole style of thought and action they had adopted. In the judgement of one researcher:

Composed primarily of young intellectual community activists, students, professionals, and aspiring jouurnalists, CASA's new leaders were in effect estranged from the mass membership which they claimed to represent. Although CASA's new leaders groped for a viable plan for the organization's consolidation and expansion [,] their growing preoccupation with developing the "correct" political position on various key issues ironically prevented further growth, and alienated the organization from much of its former community support. . . . In practice, dogmatic adherence to CASA's vision of socialist revolution lost them the popular support critical for the organization's survival. CASA's strident ideological positions also made it increasingly difficult to forge and maintain linkages with other Chicano-oriented political organizations (Gutierrez, 1982:27–28).

Needless to say, this particular sectarian style is not something inherent in socialist ideology, but is rather a result of the way in which American Marxist-Leninist groups have chosen to interpret revolutionary history. If such a style was universal, there would be many fewer successful revolutions in the modern world.

RETRADITIONALIZATION: THE NATIONAL COUNCIL OF LA RAZA AND ALINSKY-STYLE ORGANIZATIONS

As the crest of the Chicano Movement passed in the 1970s, the traditional political organizations reasserted themselves. Those groups that had their origins prior to the 1960s, such as LULAC, MAPA, and the G.I. Forum, resumed their prior importance after a period of relative eclipse. At the same time, new groups appeared that had their roots in 1960s' activism, but unlike the radical groups just discussed, pursued a course that might be termed neotraditional. While the rhetoric of some of these groups obscured their true nature, in essence they represented a continuity with the liberal reformism that has dominated Chicano politics since the time of the New Deal.[3]

The National Council of La Raza

One such organization is the National Council of La Raza, originally organized as the Southwest Council of La Raza in 1968, the same year that gave birth to CASA. Conceived as a self-consciously "moderate" organization (Sierra, 1982:157), the Southwest Council embodied the classic integrationist approach to achieving equality for Chicanos. As Christine Sierra has documented in an extensive

study of this organization, the Council was founded "in recognition
of the fact that the Americans of Mexican or Hispanic ancestry, as
a whole, have not entered into full participation in the social, civic,
political and economic life of our country, with all its benefits and
obligations" (from its initial proposal, cited in Sierra, 1982:164).

Drawing from the ideas of the eminent Chicano scholar and activist, Ernesto Galarza, who served as consultant to the organization, the Southwest Council began its efforts with community organization and mobilization as its principal orientation (Sierra,
1982:163–68). Concretely, this was to translate into such activities
as voter registration, the creation of linkages among organizations,
and research and dissemination of information. The council was to
function as a link, working through local affiliates (Sierra, 1982:164).
However, the emphasis very quickly switched to that of economic
development projects, which was more in line with the preferences of its first funding agency, the Ford Foundation (ibid., 173).
While community organization was not completely neglected, more
effort was put into such programs as a Chicano small-business investment corporation and various housing projects. Overtures were
made to large corporations, such as McDonald's and ITT-Sheraton.

Thus, even the mildly progressive initial focus soon came to be
displaced by the pressure of harsh reality, in this case in the form
of the funding agency and its conception of brown capitalism.

The Southwest Council's economic development efforts bore little fruit, however, and in 1972, the Ford Foundation began to
develop a direct relationship with the council's more viable affiliates, the Spanish-Speaking Unity Council in Oakland and the Mexican American Unity Council in San Antonio. With its rationale for
existence rapidly dissolving, the Southwest Council decided to redefine itself. In 1973, it changed its name to the National Council
of La Raza and declared that henceforth, it would function at the
national level. Its chosen roles now would be political advocacy in
Washington for Chicano causes, the monitoring of political developments in the nation's capital, and the playing of a broker, or
middleman role, between Chicano organizations and national
agencies (ibid., 194–195, 227). Although attempting to carry on a
wide range of activities, it did not do so in a very effective manner,
and the ties it has tried to establish with its "affiliates" have remained tenuous (ibid., 231).

In her overall assessment of the council's efforts, Christine Sierra states that

the strategy of community economic development "depoliticized" barrio activism and thrust the economics of small capitalism into change-oriented agendas. Since tangible products constituted the measure of success, community activists adhered to the politics of pragmatism to see that their effort produced results. . . . [C]ommunity development efforts appear to reinforce existing economic and power relationships rather than challenge them. . . . [S]uch efforts tend to promote acceptance of the tenets of liberal capitalism rather than enhance the development of alternative, creative approaches to the acquisition of political and economic power (ibid., 271–73).

ALINSKY-STYLE ORGANIZATIONS

The influence that the Saul Alinsky school of organizing has had on Chicano politics has generally not been recognized, but it is extensive. Cesar Chavez, as mentioned above, was brought into the political arena by an organizer from Alinsky's Industrial Areas Foundation. The same organizer, Fred Ross, played a key role in the creation of the Community Service Organization in Los Angeles. The Mission Coalition Organization, an important Chicano community group in San Francisco in the early seventies, was also based on the Alinsky model (Ortiz, 1984:2–4). From all parts of the Southwest, Chicano activists have journeyed to Chicago to learn organizing at the Industrial Areas Foundation training center and have returned to their communities to apply those lessons.

Saul Alinsky originally developed his concept of community organizing while working with poor Polish-Americans in Chicago's slums. The model that was born there was spelled out in Alinsky's *Reveille for Radicals,* originally published in 1946 and later updated in his *Rules for Radicals* (1972). Alinsky was committed to organizing the poor to give them greater power over their lives so that they might use that power to improve their life situations. Activating the poor would create more cohesive communities and lead to greater participation in the political process, thus furthering democratic goals.

Although Alinsky never tired of describing himself as a radical, there is nothing particularly radical in his goals. "When organizing around concrete, self-interest-oriented issues within neighborhoods, Alinsky groups usually fight not for anything resembling radical goals, but rather tend to advance ideas about preservation which smack of Burkean conservatism" (Levine, 1973:282). While one could argue that the active involvement of the poor in running their lives would in fact be a radical change from the current state of affairs, Alinsky-style organizing tends to confine itself to limited goals that do not get to the core relationships that perpetuate inequality. Its use of creative and unconventional tactics give the Alinsky approach a militant image, but its main strength lies in having a thought-out process of organizing laid out in a clear manner.

In essence, the Alinsky model consists of a few relatively straightforward elements, of which the major ones are these:

(a) sending organizers into disadvantaged communities to conduct detailed interviews, with the objectives of identifying specific issues that can be used for organizing, and of finding indigenous "natural leaders" who can be recruited

(b) pulling together an "organization of organizations," a coalition of previously existing groups, usually relying heavily on religious bodies

(c) building an initial campaign around achievable, short-term goals that can be used to create momentum and enthusiasm

(d) maintaining a flexible stance, adjusting the group's tactics in a fluid manner to the evolving level of conflict (Pruger and Specht, 1969). There is also a great deal of emphasis on organizers familiarizing themselves with local customs and traditions so that their appeals and tactics will be culturally appropriate.

Although Alinsky's tactics have been successful in many communities in making specific improvements, in practice, the approach tends to be self-limiting. In part, this is because included in the original Alinsky package is a self-consciously "nonideological" position, in which any analysis of the society that attempts to link social problems with social structure is put down as dogmatic and restricting (see, for example, Alinsky, 1969:xiii). In many ways, the Alinsky experience is virtually a textbook example of the rarely appreciated maxim that any organization lacking a true alternative vision of society will fall back on some version of the officially established truth, which inevitably reflects the viewpoint of the dominant groups.

The Chicano organizations that adopted the Alinsky model did not fall into the trap that befell the National Council of La Raza early on, that of abandoning grassroots mobilization in favor of an elite economic-development focus. However, their apparent successes are somewhat deceptive in giving the impression that there is more happening than is actually the case.

Communities Organized for Public Service (COPS)

COPS, based in San Antonio's barrios, recently celebrated its tenth anniversary, making it "the longest lived and most successful of the many community organizations inspired by the teachings of the late Saul Alinsky" (Skerry, 1984:21). It came into existence in 1974, initially through the efforts of Alinsky organizer Ernesto Cortes, a native of San Antonio. From the beginning, COPS has been strongly influenced by the Catholic church. Cortes's salary was at first paid by members of the church hierarchy, and COPS is still organized largely along parish lines (Garcia, 1980:22, 24). As one writer notes, "In the thirty parishes that have joined, COPS functions effectively as the bargaining agent to politicians. . . . In return, COPS assesses each member parish['s] dues, which in many instances come right off the top of each Sunday's collection (Skerry, 1984:21).

Through its standard Alinsky interviewing technique, COPS' organizers identified such issues as street drainage, utility rates, and the installation of sidewalks as specific starting points. From there, they have broadened their agenda to more political issues, such as campaign finance reform and the changeover of city council elections from at-large to single-member districts (Garcia, 1980:22, 24; Skerry, 1984:21, 22). COPS also plays an important role in San Antonio politics through endorsement of local candidates, and it has come to exercise considerable control over the allocation of federal community-development block grants.

Rather than remaining an isolated organization, COPS has entered into a coalition with newer Alinsky groups in other Texas cities, including Austin, Forth Worth, El Paso, and Houston, and the Rio Grande valley. Collectively, the coalition is known as Texas Interfaith. COPS also maintains close ties with the parent Alinsky organization, the Industrial Areas Foundation (IAF). Currently, Cortes is one of four members of the "cabinet" that advises the national IAF director (Skerry, 1984:22). Through these connections, COPS has been able to play a significant role in Texas politics, where Chicanos have become a more self-conscious voting bloc in recent years.

United Neighborhoods Association (UNO)

The success of COPS quickly spawned another Alinsky organization in the Chicano areas of Los Angeles. If anything, UNO's connections with the church were even tighter than those of COPS. Catholic clergy took the lead in 1975 in forming an Inter-Religious Sponsoring Committee, which raised the funds to pay Alinsky organizers to establish a COPS-type organization in Los Angeles. Ernesto Cortes was brought in from San Antonio to spearhead the effort. According to Isidro Ortiz's interpretation, UNO was brought into being as part of the local Catholic church's need to strengthen its position among Los Angeles Chicanos at a time when the church was being heavily criticized for not doing enough in the social arena. As he puts it, "The reform program emerged out of the Catholic Church's efforts to maintain its legitimacy and influence in the Chicano community in the wake of a decline in the Church's legitimacy and the emergence of threats and challenges to the Church's authority and posture on activism on behalf of Chicanos" (Ortiz, 1984:8).

By 1977, an organization had been brought into being, and interviews had been conducted that singled out the following issue areas for special attention:

1. the need for street lights, stop signs and other traffic and safety controls throughout East Los Angeles;
2. several issues in the area of police-community relations, including the need for additional police in some areas, quicker response times, and crackdowns on gang activity and drug trafficking;
3. absentee landlords who neglected their holdings in East Los Angeles;

4. the poor quality of education in schools throughout East Los Angeles; and

5. better services and higher quality goods at local stores and businesses (ibid., 23).

However, its first major campaign was based on the issue of insurance "redlining," under which residents of the East Los Angeles barrios were paying exorbitant rates for their automobile insurance compared to other residential areas. Through the efforts of UNO, these rates were significantly reduced (Torres, 1980:23). By taking up these kinds of practical and specific issues, UNO was able to mobilize grass-roots Chicanos and Chicanas who would have resisted joining many other types of organizations (Torres, 1980:23; Ortiz, 1984:24–25).

An Assessment

The Alinsky-style organizations are in a way the opposite side of the coin from the sectarians. Whereas sectarian groups are self-consciously ideological, Alinskyites are self-consciously nonideological, or at least profess to be so. Sectarians are generally out of touch with the people they hope to organize, while the Alinsky organizers are very much in tune with the person on the street. Nevertheless, the limitations of the Alinsky groups, however different, are as real and as significant as those of the sectarians.

Many of those limitations are built into the original Alinsky approach and have been carried on from organizational generation to generation. One has to do with the nature of the organizational goals, which generally remain at a very specific level and deal only with secondary issues, however real these may be on a day-to-day basis. In the case of COPS, a move toward increasingly important areas and toward a broader geographical scope has been made, but even here the demands essentially boil down to an equal share of political power for Mexican Americans. The actual structure of power or economic relationships in the society are not raised as issues, nor do they seem to be present even in an implicit way in the minds of the organizers. In the ultimate analysis, the goals are those of the traditional organizations: racial equality via integration into the dominant institutions of the society. Only the methods are different, and the methods are in a sense politically neutral and can be used for whatever political purpose. As one writer has pointed out with respect to a Chicago-area Alinsky organization:

> On occasion, Alinsky groups behave in a clearly racist fashion: one Alinsky group is dedicated to preventing Blacks from crossing a major boundary street in their neighborhood. This has been the major raison d'être of the organization since its founding, though the words used are highly coded and never publicly racist (Levine, 1973:282).

Another major limitation of these organizations has to do with the historically close association between the Industrial Areas Foundation and the churches. Following this tradition, both COPS and UNO are closely intertwined with the Catholic hierarchies in their areas, relying on them for funding, legitimacy, and an organizational base. Although there are individual priests who are willing to entertain ideas about fundamental social restructuring, the Catholic church as an institution is certainly not about to do so. As Peter Skerry has pointed out, the marriage between the IAF and the church is not simply one of convenience:

> . . . also important are the personal values of I. A. F. organizers themselves, a good number of whom come from conservative ethnic Catholic backgrounds. I. A. F.'s stance reflects a long-standing affinity between Alinsky's approach and Catholic social teaching, dating back to Alinsky's first organizing efforts in the 1930s, in Chicago's Catholic parishes, and continuing with his association with the neo-Thomist philosopher Jacques Maritain. . . .
> . . . there is a genuine religious dimension to I. A. F. organizing. For though it uses the organizational life of churches for its own ends, I. A. F. has in turn allowed itself to be influenced by the churches. Ten years ago I. A. F. went into parishes and immediately began organizing around political issues. But in recent years its organizers have moved toward theological reflection, to the point where they have developed a series of Bible study classes to get prospective members thinking about the spiritual life of their parish (Skerry, 1984:23).

CONCLUSION

With the decline of the Chicano Movement, the politics of the Mexican American people fragmented and diverged. Radical organizations sprang up that attempted to redefine Chicano politics and its goals. Traditional organizations bounced back after a period of relative obscurity and gained new recruits. New organizations also emerged on the scene that essentially shared the goals of the traditional organizations but adopted somewhat different tactics. Of these neotraditional groups, the most important were based on the organizing strategies of Alinsky and the Industrial Areas Foundation.

Looking at the period as a whole, and recognizing the distinctly secondary role of radical organizations, the most significant trend was the renewed emphasis on achieving equality for Chicanos within United States society. While there was some disagreement on the definition of "equality" and on strategies for achieving it, the most common stance was some variation on the traditional "integrationist" approach. Equality through integration meant moving Chicanos up the economic, social, and political hierarchies that are the backbone of American society.

The communitarian goal was not abandoned by postmovement organizations, but little or no analysis has been done by these groups as to what would be necessary to maintain a viable Chicano community life into the indefinite future. The underlying assumption seems to be that if equality can be achieved, the distinctive Chicano collective identity will somehow take care of itself. In the next section, I argue that this assumption is dead wrong.

NOTES

1. The *History of CASA* is a sixty-eight page manuscript written as a CASA internal document around 1978. Although anonymous, it was clearly written by one or more persons who remained in CASA after two splits had fatally weakened the organization.

2. This does not count the Partido Liberal Mexicano (PLM) of the anarchist Flores Magon brothers, active in the U.S. Southwest during the Mexican Revolution. The PLM was basically a Mexican organization, and its political focus was on Mexico.

3. Liberal reform aims at strictly limited changes that alleviate specific problems, but leaves intact the underlying structure of society.

II

A COMPARATIVE
ANALYSIS

6

Unintended Consequences
and Internal Contradictions

INTRODUCTION

If there is an overriding factor in Chicano history, it is the presence of a pervasive and institutionalized system of discrimination affecting all aspects of social life. In the economic realm, this system has taken such forms as dual wages (unequal pay for the same work) and occupational stratification (certain jobs more or less "reserved" for Chicanos and other jobs off-limits).[1] In the political arena, a parallel system has been effected through such mechanisms as gerrymandering and poll taxes. In education, it has taken the form of segregated schools and unequal resources. In housing, racial covenants were used in many places to keep Chicanos out of certain parts of town, by requiring Anglos purchasing homes to promise not to resell their properties to non-Anglos. The list goes on and on. Some scholars have used the term "internal colonialism" to refer to this generalized system.

The pattern of institutional discrimination and segregation was applied to Chicanos in the nineteenth century. Similar patterns had been created for blacks and Native Americans earlier. It was partly motivated by a perception of self-interest on the part of some sectors of the Anglo population, and partly out of prejudice. As shown in earlier chapters, this system became the main target of

Chicano political activists after the 1920s as they focused on the goal of equality.

One of the historical ironies in all this is that the barriers erected against Chicanos had the effect of reinforcing Mexican cultural patterns by preventing Chicanos from fully participating in the mainstream social and cultural life of the United States (San Miguel, 1984:205). This was an unintended consequence of the system of institutional discrimination. Indeed, the reinforcement of Mexican culture ran directly counter to the dominant cultural attitudes, which centered around the Americanization of "foreign" groups and disdain and intolerance for non-Anglo cultures.

Institutionalized discrimination also led eventually to the creation of alternative Chicano identities, and particularly to such youth subcultures as the pachuco or zootsuiter of the 1940s, and the cholo and lowrider of the 1970s and 1980s (see Plascencia, 1983: Madrid, 1972).

As we have seen, Chicano political struggles were aimed at breaking the patterns of discrimination in order to provide access to the dominant institutions and to allow individual upward mobility to take place. This essentially integrationist effort has succeeded in part, aided considerably by a number of developments in American society since the 1930s, particularly the New Deal reforms and the labor shortages created by World War II (see Barrera, 1979:Chapter 5). The rapid urbanization of Chicanos in this century has also played an important role.

Since the changes in the status of Chicanos have taken place over several decades, their significance has not always been fully appreciated. Nevertheless, their impact has been substantial. Integration into the dominant institutions is taking place, and greater economic mobility is part of that picture. One consequence of this mobility is greater class differentiation within the Chicano population, as is generally recognized.

However, there is another important consequence to these changing patterns, one that many in the Chicano community refuse to recognize or acknowledge. It represents the second historical irony: as the institutionalized barriers slowly erode, so do the cultural patterns that they have played a major role in maintaining. The contradiction here is that the partial achievement of the egalitarian goal has further undermined the prospect for attaining the communitarian goal. Far from being resolved, the dilemma that this creates has not been clearly perceived or addressed by the Chicano political leadership.

Restated, my main contentions are these:

(1) the historic Chicano ethnic goals have been equality and community
(2) Chicano political organizations since the 1920s have put their primary emphasis on achieving equality through integration and individual mobility
(3) the partial success of this effort has had the (at least ostensibly) unintended consequence of speeding up the assimilation process, and thereby undermining the goal of community.

The first two points have been discussed in chapters 2 through 5. In the remainder of this chapter, I will document the third point by examining economic status, residential patterns, language use, and rates of intermarriage.

ECONOMIC MOBILITY

Measuring the economic status of the Chicano population over time is made difficult by a number of factors. One is the problem of identifying the relevant population. Does it include all persons of Mexican origin regardless of generation? What about persons of mixed parentage? Another set of problems stems from the fact that the U.S. Census Bureau has not been consistent over the decades in how it identifies this group. Recognizing these and other imperfections in our information, it is still possible to say that the economic status of Chicanos was on the rise from 1930 to 1970, whether measured by occupational status or by income level.[2]

Detailed discussions of occupational status for Chicanos in the Southwest (California, Texas, New Mexico, Arizona, and Colorado) have been presented elsewhere (Barrera, 1979; Briggs, Fogel, and Schmidt, 1977). The general pattern has been one of a slow but distinct upward shift in the occupational status of Chicanos. In 1970, for example, Chicano males and females were still underrepresented in professional and technical occupations, but much less so than had been the case in 1930. By 1970, Chicanos in the Southwest were actually overrepresented in the skilled-worker category, whereas in 1930, they were quite underrepresented (Barrera, 1979:131; Briggs, Fogel, and Schmidt, 1977:76–77). Income data show the same general trend. In 1959, the median income of Spanish-surname males in the Southwest was 63 percent of that of Anglo males. By 1969, it had risen to 66 percent. The median income of Spanish-surname females rose from 67 percent to 76 percent of that of all females during that same time period (Briggs, Fogel, and Schmidt, 1977:61).

It would be possible to go into a great deal more detail on these trends, but my purpose here has been simply to establish the general direction of change and to give some feeling for its pace. Clearly, that change has been slow, and considerable inequality persists. Still, the position of Chicanos in the overall occupational structure is quite different now from what it was in 1930.

As one might expect, the level of formal education of Chicanos has also risen over the same period, although again, there is a long way to go and significant regional disparity (Briggs, Fogel, and Schmidt, 1977:20; Featherman and Hauser, 1978:462; Grebler, Moore, and Guzman, 1970:150–51; Jaffe, Cullen, and Boswell, 1980:91–93; 135ff).

RESIDENTIAL PATTERNS

Folk wisdom has it that as you move up (economically), you move out (of the ethnic neighborhood). As it turns out, Chicanos are no exception to the general rule.

The question of the relationship of social class to residential area was one that was taken up in the massive study published in 1970 as *The Mexican-American People* (Grebler, Moore, and Guzman, 1970). The authors examined segregation patterns in thirty-five southwestern cities and then zeroed in on Los Angeles and San Antonio for more intensive analyses. In Los Angeles, for example, they found a clear relationship between residential patterns and income levels. In 1965, 50 percent of Los Angeles Chicanos with incomes over $6,000 lived in areas with less than 15 percent Spanish-surname residents. Only 21 percent of Chicanos at that income level lived in areas of high Spanish-surname concentration. At lower income levels, the situation was reversed (ibid., 327).

A more recent study used 1970 census data to study patterns of

Spanish-American segregation in the following metropolitan areas: Chicago, Dallas, Denver, Houston, Los Angeles, Miami, San Diego, San Francisco, San Jose, and Washington, D.C. (Massey, 1979a:1017). The "Spanish-American" designation is based on the census categories of Spanish surname and Spanish language. This study clearly showed that at higher socioeconomic levels, Spanish-Americans were much less likely to be segregated from whites than was true at lower socioeconomic levels, whether measured on the basis of income, occupation, or education (ibid., 1017–18). The author's conclusions are fully consistent with the argument I am presenting here: "the implications of the above results with respect to future trends in residential segregation and assimilation of Spanish Americans are clear. Socioeconomic advancement should lead to significantly reduced levels of residential segregation among Spanish Americans, and ultimately to greater assimilation" (ibid., 1021).

In another study using 1970 census data, Matre and Mindiola examined forty-six metropolitan areas in the Southwest and found that Anglo-Chicano residential segregation was less where there was greater income equality between the two groups (Matre and Mindiola, 1981:25).

The trend is further confirmed by what has been happening over time and among different generations. One study, based on 237 U.S. metropolitan areas, found that residential segregation between "Hispanics" and whites had declined considerably from 1960 to 1970 (Van Valey, Woods, and Marston, 1982:30). Another study determined that Spanish Americans of the first and second generation are considerably more segregated from the white population than are those of the third and subsequent generations (Massey, 1979a:559).

Interestingly enough, these studies point out a sharp contrast between patterns of Latino-Anglo and black-Anglo segregation. In the first place, Latino-Anglo segregation is significantly less than black-Anglo segregation (Grebler, Moore, and Guzman, 1970:277; Massey, 1979b:557; Matre and Mindiola, 1981:20). Second, while Latino-Anglo segregation declines with increasing income levels, the same is not true for black-Anglo segregation (Massey, 1979a:1017–18). Third, the move from central cities to suburbs makes much more difference for Latino-Anglo than black-Anglo segregation (Massey, 1979b:558–59). Thus, the barriers to Chicano residential mobility appear to be lower than those that blacks confront.

In summary, then, it seems clear that the residential segregation patterns of Chicanos are breaking down. There are multiple causes of this trend, including, in many cases, urban policies destructive of the traditional barrios.[3] However, a major factor in the urban dispersion of Chicanos is the increased geographical mobility that goes with economic mobility. The two types of mobility in turn are associated with other aspects of assimilation, as has been recognized for other ethnic groups for some time. Stanley Lieberson, for example, published a study based on 1930 and 1950 census data for ten ethnic groups in ten major U.S. cities. He found a strong association between degree of segregation and such factors as language use and intermarriage (Lieberson, 1961). More recently, Amado Padilla found that Mexican Americans who had higher income levels and lived in low-ethnic-density neighborhoods scored lower on scales of cultural awareness and ethnic loyalty than individuals who had lower income levels and lived in higher-ethnic-density neighborhoods (barrios). The cultural awareness and ethnic loyalty scales were considered to be measures of acculturation (Padilla, 1980:77).

In the next two sections of this chapter, the relationship of mobility to language patterns and to intermarriage will be explored in greater detail.

LANGUAGE PATTERNS

Language use is perhaps the single best indicator of ethnic maintenance or assimilation, but it is also an exceedingly difficult area because of the complex relationship it has to various dimensions of social life. Fortunately, a great deal of work on Chicano sociolinguistics has been carried out since the 1960s, and it is possible on the basis of this literature to make some observations about trends.

In the first place, there is agreement among researchers that anglicization, the shift from Spanish to English, is taking place among the Chicano population. Gilles Grenier, for instance, analyzed data from the 1976 national Survey of Income and Education (SIE) to find that less than half of all Mexican Americans who grew up in Spanish-speaking homes were still using English as their usual language of communication (Grenier, 1984:541–42). Many of these individuals, of course, continued to use Spanish also. Another study based on the same data broke down the U.S. Spanish-mother-tongue respondents into foreign born and native born and found that 29 percent of the foreign born and 64 percent of the native born reported English as their usual language (Veltman, 1980:18–20).

As one might expect, there is considerable regional variation. In California, 79 percent of the native born whose mother tongue was Spanish identified English as their usual language, whereas in Texas, the corresponding figure was 40 percent, and in New Mexico 51 percent. The highest anglicization rate was reported in the Rocky Mountain region, with a figure of 84 percent (ibid., 22). The author states: "These data oblige us to conclude that Spanish as a dominant first language is rapidly disappearing in the United States" (ibid., 23).[4]

The sociologist David Lopez comes to very similar conclusions based on his study of language use in Los Angeles. He accounts for the fact that the situation is not widely understood in the following way:

Mass immigration from Mexico is not only more recent than European mass immigrations; it is also continuing. The waves of European mass immigration declined to a trickle after the 1920's, while the ebb and flow from Mexico have persisted and recently been a steady and increasing flow. This . . . is one (though not the only) key to understanding the appearance of language maintenance as well as other aspects of Chicano distinctiveness.

. . . the inescapable conclusion is that were it not for new arrivals from Mexico, Spanish would disappear from Los Angeles nearly as rapidly as more European immigrant languages vanished from cities in the East (Lopez, 1978:269, 276).

Language, Generation, and Age

Various studies have reported that relative proficiency in Spanish and English in the Southwest is related to the age of the respondents. In their 1975 study of an Albuquerque barrio, for example, Hudson-Edwards and Bills divided their respondents into an over-26 and an under-26 age group. Of those whose age was over 26, 90 percent reported Spanish as their mother tongue, 87 percent rated their fluency in Spanish as good or very good, and 44 percent rated their fluency in English as good or very good. In the under-26 group, only 38 percent reported Spanish as their mother tongue, 31 percent considered their Spanish as good or very good, and 86 percent rated their English as good or very good. Some 74 percent of the over-26 group but only 12 percent of the under-26 group reported Spanish as their primary home language (Hudson-Edwards and Bills, 1980:143, 147, 149, 151). Floyd reports a similar correlation between age and language use in her study of Spanish maintenance in Colorado (Floyd, 1982:300). Calvin Veltman presents detailed state-by-state and regional graphs showing that the younger age groups among the Spanish-mother-tongue population in the United States are rapidly shifting from Spanish as the usual language to English as the usual or exclusive language (Veltman, 1980:27–33). This age-related language pattern was also found by Skrabanek and by Thompson in different parts of Texas (Skrabanek, 1970; Thompson, 1971).

Perhaps a better picture of the process of language shift can be seen by examining its relationship to generational status. In this discussion, first generation refers to persons living in the United States but born in another country, second generation refers to the U.S.-native-born children of immigrants, and third generation refers to all subsequent generations unless otherwise noted.

One of the most influential studies to focus on generation was conducted by David Lopez in 1973 on more than one thousand Los Angeles County Chicano couples. He found, for example, that 84 percent of his sample of married Chicanas of the first generation currently used Spanish as their usual home language. By the second generation, this figure had dropped to 15 percent, and by the third generation, the figure was only 4 percent (Lopez, 1978:270; see also D. Lopez 1982b:41). A 1976 study of Chicano students at the University of California at San Diego showed a strong and direct relationship between later generation status and declining proficiency in Spanish (Sanchez, 1983:42–43).

Another widely cited study was carried out in 1971 in Texas, an area often considered the heartland of Chicano Spanish. In this study, Thompson found that the percentage of Chicano parents in Austin who spoke Spanish to their children dropped off markedly from the first to the third generation (Thompson, 1971:51). Significantly, Thompson found that generation in the sense of belonging to an *urban* generation in the United States was also a crucial factor in determining language use. If Chicano parents were products of a rural upbringing in the United States, they were as likely to speak Spanish to their children as parents who had been brought up in Mexico (ibid., 63–65; 74–75). Both groups were very different in this respect from parents who had been raised in the urban environment of Austin. He goes on to comment on his respondents' attitudes and practices regarding their children's learning of Spanish:

Although 76 percent of the fathers interviewed feel that Spanish is not necessary for ethnic identity, 70 percent want their children to learn Spanish. However, they do not think that the children need to learn Spanish at home. Only 20 percent encourage their children to speak Spanish around the house and over 60 percent of the children speak only English when at home. . . .

Even though the majority of the Mexican-American children are learning English as their first language and are speaking English around the home, the parents do not feel that the children are rejecting Spanish. Only 10 percent think that Spanish will die out with their children. Instead they believe that their children will automatically learn Spanish outside the home as they grow up in a Mexican-American environment (ibid., 109).

Since at least 40 percent of the adult population is in the urban first generation, parents are probably correct in assuming that their children will learn some Spanish as they contact the first generation within their neighborhood, at school, and at work. . . . However, as time goes on the urban third generation becomes a larger proportion of the population. . . . The likelihood of prolonged contact with Spanish speakers outside the home, especially within the peer group, lessens. Because the third-generation is likely to move into higher educational and occupational groups where there are fewer of the urban first generation, prolonged contact is even more unlikely (ibid., 117–18).

If the influx of rural Mexican-Americans were to halt, within one more generation Spanish would disappear (ibid., 116).

Language and Socioeconomic Status

The relative use of Spanish and English is also affected by the various measures of socioeconomic status, whether these be income, occupation, or level of formal education. In one study, Jon Amastae found that southern Texas Chicano college-students with higher-income fathers were more likely to have spoken English as their first language, although the relationship to the mothers' incomes was not as clear-cut (Amastae, 1982:270). Penalosa and McDonagh noted in their 1961 study of Pomona, California, that upward mobility among the Mexican American respondents was positively associated with the use of English rather than Spanish (Penalosa and McDonagh, 1966:503).

Thompson, in his previously cited Texas study, found that the tendency to speak Spanish to one's children declined with increasing education and occupational status, even with controls for respondents' place of upbringing. (Thompson, 1971:74, 87, 94, 97). David Lopez reports that his Los Angeles sample shows declining Spanish maintenance with higher levels of education, occupational status, and income (Lopez, 1978:274–75). Analysis of data from the 1979 Current Population Survey showed similar results (Lopez, 1982:54, 56).

Skrabanek also notes the reinforcing effects of residential and class factors for his Texas respondents: "Data . . . indicated that those Mexican-American youngsters growing up in the study area who speak mostly English, attain the highest levels of education, possess the highest incomes and are in the highest status occupations tend to move away from the area to large population centers where there are comparatively fewer Mexican-Americans" (Skrabanek, 1970:278).

Finally, Mirowsky and Ross conducted a survey of 194 Mexican Americans in El Paso in 1975 and found that those respondents with higher socioeconomic status tended to participate less in Spanish language networks than those of lower status (Mirowsky and Ross, 1984:561).

Language Maintenance: Conclusion

Stanley Lieberson and his associates published a study in 1975 comparing trends in linguistic diversity in thirty-five countries over various time periods spanning the nineteenth and twentieth centuries. They found two major factors that strongly influenced the degree of diversity over time. One was spatial isolation of the linguistic groups, which they hypothesized operated through the mechanism of social isolation: "Social isolation would result in more contact with linguistic compatriots, less pressure to acquire and use some other language, and therefore a lower rate of mother-tongue change between generations" (Lieberson, Dalto, and Johnston, 1975:42). The other important factor was official language policy, indicated by the degree to which the various languages within a country were used for instruction in the schools (ibid., 46). The aspect of this analysis dealing with social isolation has been pursued by Rosaura Sanchez in her review of Chicano bilingualism.

If culture is the sum of experiences and traditions held in common by a group of people, one can find different "cultures" within the Chicano population, determined by socio-economic class, residence in urban or rural areas, residence in barrios or integrated communities, generation in the United States, and nativity. Spanish is closely tied to culture for the low-income, first- and second-generation, working-class Chicanos in town barrios. For them Spanish is still the language of restaurants, filling stations, small grocery stores, bakeries, tortillerias, parks and community centers. In urbanized barrios adjacent to industrial zones, traversed by innumerable freeways, the language bonds are weakened. English becomes the language of the Anglo-owned supermarkets, the shopping centers, the drugstores, the white-bread bakeries, the filling stations, the community clinics and the fast-food drive-ins. . . .

The occupational shifts of this century, converting Chicanos into an urban blue-collar and service-workers population, has undoubtedly increased contact with English speakers in factories and the service sector, reducing thereby interactional segregation. The linguistic picture of the Southwest is thus as complex as the occupational, economic and social situation.

To the degree then that Chicanos have been isolated or set apart, economically and socially, they have maintained ample use of their Spanish-language varieties. To the degree that they have been incorporated into English-dominant employment categories and moved up the income scale, they have been acculturated, probably moved out of the barrio and into integrated communities and lost significant use of the Spanish language, with almost exclusive use of the English language (Sanchez, 1983:59–60).

According to the comparative study by Calvin Veltman cited earlier, there is only one place in English-speaking North America where a language other than English is holding its own, and that is in Quebec. It is no coincidence that that is also the only place where the non-Anglo population is large enough and concentrated enough to establish the linguistic climate, and where it has been able to set official language policy through its control of a regional government. The case of the Quebecois will be explored in greater detail in Chapter 7.

INTERMARRIAGE

Intermarriage is generally taken as a good indicator of the degree to which a particular group is assimilating into the social structure of the society-at-large. As used here, intermarriage will mean marriage between a Chicano and a non-Chicano.

Figures from the 1970 U.S. Census indicate that in that year, 16 percent of Spanish-origin males and 17 percent of Spanish-origin females were married to persons not of Spanish origin (Murguia and Cazares, 1982:94). Another body of data derived from the Census Bureau's Current Population Surveys has the advantage of being able to distinguish persons of Mexican heritage. The information for the years 1976 to 1980 has been tabulated into a five-year average by Arce and Abney. For the United States as a whole, they found a 15.9 percent intermarriage rate for Mexican-origin males and a 16.5 percent rate for females. For the Southwest, the corresponding figures were 12.3 percent and 12.5 percent and for nonsouthwestern states, they were 36.9 percent and 39.4 percent (Arce and Abney, 1982:3).

Still another estimate comes from the 1979 national survey conducted by the Institute for Social Research at the University of Michigan. As reported by Armando Abney-Guardado, this survey found that 17.6 percent of Mexican-origin males and 19.7 percent of Mexican-origin females were intermarried (Abney-Guardado, 1983:83).

Beyond these aggregate figures, we find a great deal of regional variation and considerable change over time, although we must rely on scattered studies for this information. Edward Murguia has recently pulled these various works together in order to allow comparison. Within Texas, for instance, it appears that the extent of intermarriage decreases as one goes south in the state, proceeding from metropolitan San Antonio to urban Corpus Christi to the semirural Rio Grande valley, where Chicanos are very heavily concentrated. The most nearly comparable statistics show San Antonio with 16 percent Chicano intermarriage (1973), Corpus Christi with 9 percent (1970–1971), and Edinburg, a valley town, with 5 percent (1971) (Murguia, 1982:48). By contrast, New Mexico's Albuquerque had a Mexican American intermarriage rate of 24 percent in 1971. Los Angeles, with the largest urban concentration of Chicanos, weighed in with a 36 percent rate in 1970 and 34 percent in 1974. A figure of 34 percent is also reported for nearby San Bernardino for 1970–1977 (ibid., 49).

From these various figures, then, we can form the impression that rates of Chicano intermarriage are higher outside the Southwest than in the Southwest, higher in urban than more rural areas, and higher in relatively wealthy states, such as California.

The available information also points quite clearly to increasing rates of Chicano intermarriage over time. The area for which we have the longest time perspective is San Antonio, thanks to a study by Frank Bean and Benjamin Bradshaw based on Spanish surnames. They found that for the 1850–1860 period, the number of Spanish-surnamed individuals marrying outside the group was 5 percent, whereas by the 1960 period, it had risen to 11 percent (Bean and Bradshaw, 1970:394; Murguia and Frisbie, 1977:384). Murguia and Frisbie found the intermarriage rates for this area to be hovering around 14 percent to 16 percent for the 1964–1973 period (Murguia and Frisbie, 1977:384). Avelardo Valdez used similar methodology to examine the period 1971 to 1980, and observed intermarriage rates for San Antonio Chicanas ranging between 14 percent and 17 percent, while male Chicano rates rose from around 8–9 percent to around 15–17 percent (Valdez, 1983:141).

Somewhat more limited data are available for Los Angeles, where it was found by Mittelbach, Moore, and McDaniel that the proportion of Mexican Americans intermarrying in 1963 was 25 percent. This figure is contrasted with the 9 percent exogamy rate found by Panunzio for the 1924–1933 period (Mittelbach, Moore, and McDaniel, 1966:15). The figures are not for strictly comparable populations, but they do give rough idea of the trend (see Murguia, 1982:note 10).

Two studies have also shown a striking relationship between

generation and tendency to marry exogamously. Schoen, Nelson, and Collins examined California statistics and discovered that in 1966, 19 percent of Mexican American first-generation females and 14 percent of first-generation males married outside the group. For second and later generations combined, the comparable figures were 40 percent and 39 percent. They found a similar pattern for 1970 and 1974 (Schoen, Nelson, and Collins, 1978:366). The authors note that their data at first seemed to indicate a decline in intermarriage rates from 1962 to 1974, but the seeming decline owed to the fact that over that time period, the proportion of first-generation marriages had significantly increased in California. In recent decades, California has become the major destination for Mexican immigrants, whereas earlier in the century, it had been Texas.

Mittelbach, Moore, and McDaniel confined their detailed analysis of intermarriage by generation to Los Angeles County for 1963. They broke their sample down into three generations and found a considerable increase in intermarriage from first to second generation, and a further increase for third generation. First generation grooms, for example, chose their marriage partners as follows: 52 percent first-generation Mexican American, 23 percent second-generation Mexican American, 12 percent third-generation Mexican American, and 13 percent other (mostly Anglo). Third-generation grooms, by contrast, married as follows: 7 percent first-generation Mexican American, 24 percent second-generation Mexican American, 39 percent third-generation Mexican American, and 31 percent other (Mittelbach, Moore, and McDaniel, 1966:8). The authors make a point of noting that the third generation is more likely to marry Anglos than they are either first- or second-generation Mexican Americans (at least in Los Angeles).

Intermarriage rates also go up with higher socioeconomic status, whether measured through occupation, income, or education. The Mittelbach, Moore, and McDaniel study cited above shows that Mexican American men in the "high status" occupational group (professional, technical workers, managers, officials, and proprietors) had an intermarriage rate of 40 percent, which was considerably higher than the approximately 22 percent rate for middle- and lower-status occupational groups. The highest exogamy rate was for high-status third-generation males, of whom almost half married outside the group (ibid., 21). Armando Abney-Guardado found with his national sample that Chicanos with higher levels of formal education and higher incomes were more likely to intermarry (Abney-Guardado, 1983:86, 87). Abney-Guardado also found that respondents who intermarried generally rated themselves lower in Spanish-language ability than those who married within the group (ibid., 106–7).

In summary, then, we can see that a considerable amount of intermarriage is taking place, and in such a manner as to confirm the general thesis I have set forth. The rate has been increasing over time, it is strongly affected by generation and by social class, and it is related to other indices of assimilation, such as language. These figures take on added significance when compared to those of other groups. For black Americans, for instance, the exogamy rate was less than 1 percent in 1960, and still less than 1 percent in 1970. For a typical "white ethnic" group, Polish Americans, the intermarriage rate was 12 percent in 1930, 27 percent in 1950, and 50 percent in 1960. For Italians, the figures were 17 percent in 1930, 36 percent in 1950, and 56 percent in 1960. For Japanese Americans in Los Angeles, the exogamy rate was 1 percent in 1924–1933, 10 percent in 1949–1959, and 31 percent in 1971–1972 (figures cited in Murguia, 1982:38, 40, 42). The Chicano pattern thus appears to be more similar to that of "white ethnics" and Asian Americans than to blacks.

CONCLUSION

Assimilation is often discussed in terms of two components, labeled "cultural" and "structural." Structural assimilation refers to a minority group becoming integrated into the social structure of a society. Social structure in turn is subdivided into primary groups, such as the family or social cliques, and secondary groups, such as corporations, universities, or political institutions. Cultural assimilation, or acculturation, refers to a situation in which a group gradually takes on the cultural traits of another group, such as language, customs, and music (Gordon, 1964).

As we have seen, both categories of assimilation are taking place for the Chicano population. Occupational upgrading represents structural assimilation at the secondary level, while intermarriage is an aspect of assimilation at the primary group level. Language shift reflects acculturation. Residential dispersal has implications for both structural and cultural assimilation.

This entire process is, of course, strongly affected by the continued immigration of people from Mexico to the United States. The new immigrants are predominantly monolingual in Spanish, start at or near the bottom of the occupational hierarchy, tend to settle initially in barrios, and have low rates of intermarriage. A review of the data in this chapter indicates tht this massive movement of people across national boundaries has not stopped the assimilation process. Rather, it has created a syndrome that we might call pipeline assimilation. Mexican immigrants come to the United States and if they stay, enter into an assimilation process that may take four generations to complete. At any given moment, there are generational cohorts at every stage of the process.

The result is an extremely heterogeneous and very fragmented population, one that is crosscut with all kinds of internal cultural divisions. Small wonder that it has proved difficult historically to pull this group into a coherent political movement.

The assimilation process is of course a product of many societal factors. Given the situation in the United States, cultural assimilation would probably be taking place even if structural assimilation were not. However, it seems obvious that the efforts of Chicano political groups to break down the institutional barriers to mobility have been part of this process, and have had the effect of speeding it up. In effect, these groups have opted for equality over community, although it is the rare group that would state this up front, as the 1930s LULACs did.

The two historic goals, then, are not by their nature inconsistent with each other. However, they are *in effect* contradictory, given three existing conditions: (1) the strategy for attaining equality has been individual upward mobility via institutional integration; (2) equality has been implicitly or explicitly given a higher priority than community, for the most part; and (3) conditions facing Chicanos in the United States are those of a minority, subordinate group confronting a majority, dominant group.

NOTES

1. The description of these particular practices occupies much of my first book, *Race and Class in the Southwest* (1979).

2. There is some indication of a possible decline in occupational status with the economic downturn of the early 1970s, but it is difficult to tell if this represents a short-term fluctuation or a long-term trend (see Kane, 1979). The 1980 Census figures are not very useful in this respect because the Census Bureau no longer used the Spanish surname identifier that allows 1950 to 1970 comparison.

3. For a good description of this process as applied to Detroit, see Valdes, 1982.

4. David Lopez has summarized much of the language information from the 1976 Survey of Income and Education in a recent monograph (Lopez, 1982a). In this study, he presents a detailed comparison of Mexican Americans and other Spanish-origin groups.

7

Learning from Experience, Part I: Canada and China

The traditional approach of Chicano ethnic politics, I have argued, contains an inherent contradiction. Played out to its logical conclusion, it will result in the end of the group as a recognizable community. The group loses its communal identity, and the general society loses an important element of diversity. Given this prospect, what are the possible responses?

One response is simply to accept the situation, and there will be many who will choose this route, or who have already tacitly done so. The other possibility is to search for an alternative model with alternative goals, one that does not force a choice between equality and community. I have chosen this latter route, and in this chapter, I begin to explore it by looking at the experience of ethnic minorities in other countries, in order to learn from those experiences.

Since multiethnic and multiracial societies are the rule rather than the exception, one is forced to choose one's examples from a large range of possibilities. I have chosen to look at four countries: Canada (Quebec), China, Switzerland, and Nicaragua. The reasons for choosing these examples will become more obvious as the discussion progresses. Briefly, I selected countries that provide a range of experiences in a variety of circumstances, but I also focused on countries where interesting social experiments are underway. Choosing societies where matters are worse than those in the United

States would have served little purpose in searching for alternative models, so I chose countries that in some way are dealing with ethnic and racial relations in a more progressive manner. In engaging in this sort of comparative exercise, I recognize the unique aspects of each historical situation. Still, there are many common elements as well, and looking at concrete examples has the virtue of showing *possibilities* and of putting the U.S. experience in perspective. Too often Americans proceed as if the United States were the only multiethnic society in the world. The idea is not to find an ideal model to emulate uncritically but to gather ideas that might suggest useful directions for a future U.S. society.

CANADA/QUEBEC

Canada is a good starting point because of its proximity to the United States and its similarity in being a multiethnic industrial democracy. It is a country that is often cited in a negative fashion by U.S. conservatives, who like to point to Quebec as a horrible example of what might happen in the Southwest with its growing Chicano population. The Canadian case has also attracted considerable attention in ethnic studies since the 1960s, and especially since the Parti Quebecois (PQ) victory in the provincial elections of 1976. Although Canada has a number of minority ethnic and racial groups, the focus will be on the French-speaking minority, the Francophones, especially in Quebec (the Quebecois).

Population Distribution

The basic ethnic distribution of Canada can be seen in Table 7.1. Ethnicity here refers to the country of origin of oneself or one's ancestors and not to language use.

The language-use percentages are presented in Table 7.2, by province, for 1971. The four small Atlantic-region provinces are presented first, then the industrial "heartland" of Quebec and Ontario, and finally the four more agricultural and natural-resource-based western provinces.

The relative proportion of the French-origin population has remained fairly stable since Canada assumed its modern form with the Act of Confederation (British North America Act) in 1867. The

Table 7.1
Ethnic Distribution of the Canadian Population, 1901 and 1971

Origin	1901	1971
British	57.0	44.6
French	30.7	28.7
German	5.8	6.1
Italian	0.2	3.4
Ukrainian	0.1	2.2
Dutch	0.6	1.9
Scandinavian	0.6	1.8
Polish	0.1	1.4
Indian and Eskimo	2.4	1.3
Other	2.5	8.6
Total	100.0	100.0

Source: Report of the Royal Commission on Bilingualism and Biculturalism, Book 4, 1965–1971, p. 248. Reproduced with the permission of the Minister of Supply and Services Canada.

long-term trend has been for the proportion of English ethnic origin to decline, but in a sense, this has been offset by the tendency of other immigrant groups to become assimilated into the dominant culture and to become English-speaking (Anglophones) (Kalbach, 1978). This tendency to assimilate English has been true even in Montreal, Quebec's largest city, and was one of the concerns that led to the language policy changes described below.

The French were able historically to maintain their relative numerical position despite unfavorable immigration rates largely because of their high fertility rate, a phenomenon popularly referred to as "the revenge of the cradle." However, French fertility has fallen drastically since the 1950s, and by the late 1960s, Quebec had the lowest crude birth-rate of any Canadian province (ibid.,90).

The French have also remained fairly concentrated in the province of Quebec. In the 1970s, about three-fourths of Canada's Francophones were living in Quebec, where, as can be seen from Table 7.2, they constituted 80 percent of the population (Henripin, 1973:155). While non-French immigrants have often arrived in Quebec, many of them have eventually passed through the province to settle in Ontario and the other more western provinces (Joy, 1972:86).

88 *A Comparative Analysis*

Table 7.2
Population and Percentage Distribution of English, French, and Other Mother Tongues by Province, 1971

Provinces	Population	English	French	Other mother tongues
Newfoundland	522,105	98.5%	0.7%	0.8%
Prince Edward Island	111,640	92.4	6.6	1.1
Nova Scotia	788,960	93.0	5.0	2.0
New Brunswick	634,560	64.7	34.0	1.3
Quebec	6,027,760	13.1	80.7	6.2
Ontario	7,703,105	77.5	6.3	16.2
Manitoba	988,245	67.1	6.1	26.8
Saskatchewan	926,245	74.1	3.4	22.5
Alberta	1,627,875	77.6	2.9	19.5
British Columbia	2,184,620	82.7	1.7	15.5

Source: Susan Walters, ed., *Canadian Almanac & Directory*, 1975, p. 343; *Canada Year Book 1974*, p. 166; *Special Bulletin, 1971 Census of Canada, Population: Specified Mother Tongues for Census Divisions and Subdivisions*, 1972. Table adapted from Donald Smiley, "French-English Relations in Canada and Consociational Democracy," in Milton Esman, ed., *Ethnic Conflict in the Western World* (Ithaca: Cornell University Press, 1977), p. 181. Reprinted with permission.

The major trends with respect to language use and linguistic assimilation were laid out in Richard Joy's *Languages in Conflict* (1972). He notes that Canada is basically a two-language country and that the French linguistic area is centered on Quebec. The areas of neighboring Ontario and New Brunswick that have substantial francophone minorities are simply extensions of the Quebec linguistic community. Everywhere else in Canada, French speakers are assimilating English, a trend that has been noted by other researchers as well (Lieberson, 1970:35, 95; Veltman, 1980:5ff). The areas that border Quebec are a kind of bilingual buffer zone between Canada's predominantly French and predominantly English areas.

English is also the dominant language in Canada in terms of second-language use. Analysis of 1961 census data indicates that only 31 percent of the Canadian population spoke French, even though some 30 percent of the respondents were of French ethnic origin. By contrast, 80 percent were able to speak English, approximately double the number of people reporting an English ethnic origin (Joy, 1972:9). Only 5 percent of the population whose mother tongue was not French could speak French, whereas more than half of the population whose mother tongue was not English could speak English (Lieberson, 1970:33). There were many more native French speakers who knew English than there were native English speakers who knew French.

A Brief Chronology

The central area of Canada along the St. Lawrence River was originally settled by the French. In 1759, the British conquered French Canada, and in 1763, the area was formally ceded to Britain by France. The 1774 Quebec Act guaranteed to the French the right to their language, their religion, and their court system. A period of unrest and experimentation with various provincial arrangements culminated in 1867 with the Confederation that provided the basic constitutional framework for the later development of Canada. The legal statute that established that framework is known as the British North America Act, and it originally brought together four provinces, of which Quebec is one. The 1871 census showed 929,000 citizens of French origin and 243,000 of British origin in Quebec (Morton, 1981:9). Reflecting the British minority status within Quebec, the British North American Act granted the English the right to control their own schools within the province. The act also guaranteed the use of the French language along with English in the federal courts and parliament.

As other provinces were added, they became dominated by English-speaking settlers because of the prevailing immigration patterns. In 1870, for example, Manitoba was formed with two official languages and two school systems. In 1890, however, the official status of French and the French Catholic school system were abolished. Quebec remained the stronghold of French culture. Immigration out of Quebec was largely limited to the surrounding areas and to the U.S. New England area.

In the latter part of the nineteenth century, Quebec remained a relatively conservative and rural-dominated province, with a strong church influence. The most important sectors of the economy came to be in the hands of English-speaking Canadians and Americans, leading to what some analysts refer to as a "cultural division of labor" (McRoberts and Posgate, 1980). In 1936, the newly formed

Union Nationale won the Quebec provincial elections, and under their conservative leader Maurice Duplessis, they controlled the political life of the province until 1960.

During this apparently quiescent period, however, important changes were taking place that were to manifest themselves in the 1960s in what has come to be known as the Quiet Revolution. Under the steady impact of urbanization and industrialization, the prevailing arrangements and assumptions were gradually undermined, particularly those of a limited state role and a strong church influence (Guinden, 1978:228–31). With the growth of an expanded urban working-class and a new professional-managerial class emerging to manage the increasingly complex economy, the stage was set for the 1960 provincial elections (McRoberts and Posgate, 1980:99ff). In those elections, the Quiet Revolution began in earnest with the victory of the provincial branch of the Liberal party, led by the new premier Jean Lesage.

In the following decade, the role of the state and in particular the provincial bureaucracy was greatly expanded, and the traditional power of the church greatly reduced. The state came to play a much more important role in the control of the educational system and the provincial economy. The slogan of the 1960 Liberals had been "maitres chez nous" (masters in our own house), and the corollary of this appeal was the assertion of French power in relation to the anglophone-controlled federal bureaucracy and national economy (ibid.). In 1967, the Parti Quebecois (PQ) was formed in order to push the logic of French nationalism further than the Liberals were willing to do.

There was a federal response to the growing assertion of French rights, and certain concessions were made. The Royal Commission on Bilingualism and Biculturalism was established in 1963, and a number of its recommendations were translated into official federal policy in 1969. The Official Languages Act of that year specified that federal services should be available to language minorities wherever they were a sizable number, and it provides funds to the provinces for minority official-language instruction. National radio and television programs are also provided in English and French (Wardhaugh, 1983:47–48; Brazeau and Cloutier, 1977:205).

These and other concessions were not enough to stem the tide of Quebecois nationalism. In 1970, the PQ won 23 percent of the vote in Quebec provincial elections, and political kidnappings by the more radical Front pour la Liberation du Quebec (FLQ) led to the invoking of the federal War Measures Act and the temporary intervention of federal military forces. In 1973, the PQ received 30 percent of the provincial vote, compared to the Liberals' 54 percent. The following year, Quebec's Liberal government passed Bill 22, making French the official language of the province and revoking the official status that English had been given by the British North America Act (Breton, Reitz, and Valentine, 1980:240). This and later developments in language policy are described more fully in a separate section below.

In 1976, the Parti Quebecois was able to gain control of the provincial government with 41 percent of the popular vote, with the rest of the vote divided between the Union Nationale, the Liberals, and smaller parties. They used their control of the provincial assembly to pass the next major piece of language legislation, Bill 101, the Charter of the French Language. In 1980, the PQ put before the provincial voters their proposal for sovereignty-association, which would have moved Quebec toward sovereign status while maintaining certain formal relations with Canada. The wording of the referendum was as follows:

The Government of Quebec has made public its proposal to negotiate a new agreement with the rest of Canada, based on the equality of nations;

This agreement would enable Quebec to acquire the exclusive power to make its laws, levy its taxes and establish relations abroad—in other words, sovereignty—and at the same time to maintain with Canada an economic association including a common currency;

No change in political status resulting from these negotiations will be effected without approval by the people through another referendum;

On these terms, do you give the Government of Quebec the mandate to negotiate the proposed agreement between Quebec and Canada? (Jacobs, 1980: 87–88; see also McRoberts and Posgate, 1980: 229ff).

The vote on the referendum went against the PQ 60 percent to 40 percent, with the Francophone vote almost evenly divided and the Anglophone vote heavily against. In 1981, the PQ won the provincial election over the Liberal party.

In 1982, Canada passed the Constitution Act, which finally "patriated" the Canadian Constitution. The process of disengaging

Canada from Great Britain had been so long and slow that prior to 1982, the Canadian Constitution could be amended only by going through the British Parliament. The Constitution Act also made Canada constitutionally bilingual. However, the province of Quebec refused to join in signing the new constitution at this point, feeling that it did not sufficiently acknowledge Quebec's distinctive status and rights.

In 1985, René Levesque, leader of the Parti Quebecois since its founding, resigned from his position as party head after a steady decline in the popularity of the PQ and after a lengthy recession. His replacement by the pragmatic Pierre Marc Johnson was a clear sign that the high tide of Quebecois separatism had passed. In December, the Liberal party swept into power, taking 98 of the 121 seats in the provincial legislature in an election dominated by economic issues and a narrowing of ideological differences between the two major parties. Robert Bourassa became the new premier of Quebec.

In 1987, the Bourassa administration arrived at a major agreement with the Canadian federal government and the other provinces. It was agreed that Quebec would now sign the Constitution. In return, Quebec was acknowledged as the "distinct society" in Canada, with a district cultural identity. The agreement also specified that three of the nine judges on the Canadian Supreme Court would be appointed from a list of jurists provided by Quebec. In addition, the provinces as a whole were given greater powers over the regulation of immigration into the provinces, and over future constitutional amendments affecting the structure of the federal government.

Quebecois Aspirations

The goals and aspirations of the Quebecois in recent years have had a great deal in common with the goals of Chicanos described earlier. The Quebecois perceived that they were not truly "masters in their own house," and that this lack of control had resulted in an unequal economic status with respect to Canadian Anglophones. They also saw this lack of control over their own destiny as threatening their cohesion as a distinct cultural community, given various demographic trends.

The historic economic situation of the Quebecois is summarized in the following quote from a recent study:

For over two centuries Quebec has been marked by a clear cultural division of labour. This internal dependence has been based on the presence of a permanent Anglophone community in Quebec. This community has initiated and controlled much of Quebec's economic activity. The various English-speaking external interests who have become involved in Quebec's economic development had drawn heavily upon the Anglophone community for their personnel. Unlike more "foreign language" settings, such as continental Europe, Quebec offered a large pool of established, highly-qualified English-speakers; thus, there was little need for Anglophone corporations to turn to the Francophone majority, as long as they were prepared to pay a premium for Anglophone personnel. In this way, internal, cultural division of labour remained largely intact, despite changes in Quebec's external relations from its British colonial status, to its role as dominant centre of Canada, to its dependence on Ontario and the United States (McRoberts and Posgate, 1980:16).

One of the galling aspects of the provincial economy, in the eyes of the Quebecois, is that historically, its upper reaches have been controlled by Anglophones. It has been found, for instance, that only 26 of the 165 businesses in the province with an annual production over 10 million dollars are owned by French Canadians (ibid., 47). Francophone-owned establishments tend to be smaller than either Canadian-Anglophone- or foreign-owned firms, and tend to produce goods that are sold primarily within the province. English-Canadian- and foreign-owned firms are much more export-oriented (Breton, Reitz, and Valentine, 1980:154–55). Typically, the ethnicity of the owners tends to determine the ethnicity of the boards of directors and top management (Raynauld, 1973:149; Breton, Reitz, and Valentine, 1980:155). The largest firms are generally foreign-owned, typically by Americans.

Not surprisingly, the lack of economic control translates into substantially lower income figures for the Quebecois. In 1961, at the beginning of the Quiet Revolution, it was found that male employees of French origin earned only 67 percent as much as those of English origin within the metropolis of Montreal. By 1971, that figure had risen to 77 percent. Within the province as a whole, the 1961 ratio of French to English male-employee income was 64 percent (Breton, Reitz, and Valentine, 1980:148–49). Studies by Andre Raynauld indicate that the income disparaties become greater as the level of education goes up (Raynauld, 1973:147; Breton, Reitz, and Valentine, 1980:152).

Issues of cultural identity overlap with the specifically economic issues but also transcend them. Historically, French Canadians operate under the assumption that Canada was formed on the basis of two "founding peoples," of which they are one and the English the other (Jacobs, 1980:79ff). In this view, Quebec, as the homeland of one of the charter groups, occupies a special status that sets it apart from the other provinces. French culture is also seen as entitled to a special status and to protection from the threat of assimilation that is posed by its precarious position in a continent dominated by English (see Wardhaugh, 1983:Chapter 1; Arnopoulos and Clift, 1984).

Much of the Quebecois anxiety about their culture is traceable to population trends. While the overall proportion of Francophones in Canada has remained relatively stable since the last century, there are specific patterns that have worried many. One is the decline in the French birthrate, which historically has served to maintain the ethnic balance. The other is the tendency of immigrants with other cultural backgrounds to choose English over French as their home language by a ratio of three to one (Henripin, 1973:159). Even though Quebec is predominantly French-speaking, immigrants' decisions are apparently strongly influenced by the economic control exercised by Anglophones.

The cultural concerns of the Quebecois have been particularly acute with respect to Montreal, which contains a third of the province's population and is the economic and intellectual center of Quebec. It is also in Montreal where 80 percent of the province's non-French population live (ibid., 157). Historically, Montreal has been the economic center of Canada, but since mid-century, it has been displaced by Toronto. The fact that the French composition of Montreal has remained relatively stable from 1871 to 1971 at about 60 percent has not eliminated French concern for its future cultural makeup (McRoberts and Posgate, 1980:52).

From French Canadians to Quebecois

Most observers agree that over the last few decades, a shift has
occurred in the self-perception of Francophones living within Qubec.
Whereas in the past, the tendency may have been to identify with
French speakers wherever they lived in Canada, and to refer to
the group as "Canadiens," or French-Canadians, the era of the
Quiet Revolution saw a shift to an identification as Quebecois.

This reformulation of the dominant French-Canadian ideology also involved a narrowing of the boundaries of the "nation." In the past, nationalists had been ready to see the French-Canadian nation as extending
throughout much of Canada, and perhaps even extending into areas of the
northeastern United States. With the 1960's, nationalism became increasingly focused upon Quebec alone. Whatever political arrangements were
advocated, an increasing number of Quebecois refused to merge the primary identity of Quebec Francophones with that of Canada as a whole. . . .
For all intents and purposes, the "nation" and Quebec had become
same (McRoberts and Posgate, 1980:96; see also Dion, 1976:31, and Breton, Reitz, and Valentine, 1980: 207–8).

The change reflected the perception that francophone aspirations were unattainable in the country-at-large, and could best be
realized by the concentration of efforts in that area where they
constituted a majority. Within this context, the Quiet Revolution
under the Liberals represented a stage of modernizing nationalism
that was the product of a long historical process, and the PQ's
coming to power can be seen as a further stage in that process.
Although the reformist nature of this party has led to its being
labeled "social democratic," many analysts have stressed its fundamentally nationalist thrust and its somewhat ambiguous relationship with the labor union movement in order to qualify that designation (see, for example, Dion, 1976:141–43; McRoberts and
Posgate, 1980:193; Piotte and Vaillancourt, 1978:38).

The Centrality of the Language Issue

Under the Liberals and then under the Parti Quebecois, a wide
range of issues have been addressed and initiatives undertaken.

Among the areas of concern have been expanding the economic role of the state, improving social services, strengthening the role of the unions, modernizing the educational system, and upgrading the occupational status of Francophones within the private sector. However, none with the possible exception of sovereignty-association, has stirred as much debate and focused as much attention on Quebec as the issue of language rights. Language became a key issue in part because of the economic implications of language use, and in part because of the central role that it plays in cultural maintenance.

At the federal level, the government has attempted to deal with the problem by declaring both English and French to be official languages of Canada, by seeking to provide bilingual services in federal districts, by increasing the numbers of Francophones in federal positions, and by trying to persuade the provinces to follow suit. New Brunswick, however, is the only province that accords French as well as English the status of an official language (Breton, Reitz, and Valentine, 1980:238–39). The use of French as a language of instruction in the schools is very uneven and depends on the inclination of the provincial governments.

The Liberal regime that was in power in Quebec in 1974 tried to deal with the issue by passing the Official Language Act, commonly referred to as Bill 22. It declared French to be the official language of Quebec, changing the coequal status that English had enjoyed in the province since the passage of the British North America Act in 1867.

A second provision of Bill 22 attempted to deal with the fears of Francophones that the preference of immigrants for the English language threatened the cultural dominance of French in Quebec. It did this by limiting access to English-language schools to children whose mother tongue was English or who could demonstrate through tests that they already had proficiency in English (Brazeau and Cloutier, 1977:208). Unfortunately, this provision only succeeded in angering Francophones who felt it did not go far enough, as well as Anglophones and immigrants who wanted unrestricted freedom of choice to send their children to English schools.

The third major provision of the act had to do with the issue of the language used in the workplace. Given the degree of anglophone control of the Quebec economy, the pattern has been for

English to be the language of work in many sectors, particularly as one ascends the corporate hierarchy. This is perceived as a major barrier to economic mobility for French speakers, and partly accounts for their underrepresentation at the managerial level (McRoberts and Posgate, 1980:129ff; for recent improvements in this situation, see Lortie, 1981). Bill 22 addressed this issue in a halfhearted way by requiring "francization certificates" from the government, attesting to the use of French in the workplace, in order to qualify private companies for government benefits and contracts. However, the law was written in a sufficiently vague manner to allow a great deal of leeway in practice, depending on how vigorously the government chose to interpret the requirements (McRoberts and Posgate, 1980:174).

When the Parti Quebecois took over the provincial government, it pushed the language issue further with its Bill 101, passed in 1977. This bill made francization cerificates mandatory for all businesses with more than fifty employees, whereas Bill 22 has made this optional. It also stipulated that all advertising must be in French and made bilingual signs illegal except in special cases. It also established *L'Office de la langue francaise* to oversee the implementation of the law and to monitor the status of the French language in the province (Wardhaugh, 1983:94ff; Kahn, 1985:119ff; McRoberts and Posgate, 1980:209ff).

Bill 101 also went beyond Bill 22 in specifying restrictions on who could enroll in English schools. It stated that children must attend French-language schools except for those in the following categories:

(a) a child whose father or mother received his or her elementary instruction in English in Quebec;

(b) a child whose father or mother, domiciled in Quebec on the date of the coming into force of this act, received his or her elementary instruction in English outside Quebec;

(c) a child who, in his last year of school in Quebec before that coming into force of this act, was lawfully receiving his instruction in English, in a public kindergarten class or in an elementary or secondary school;

(d) younger brothers and sisters of a child described in paragraph "c" (as cited in Kahn, 1985:121–22).

These bills evoked considerable negative response from Quebec's anglophone community, leading some businesses to relocate their headquarters to Toronto and creating some emigration of English speakers from Quebec to other provinces. On balance, however, it appears that the costs of Bill 101 have not been exhorbitant (Laporte, 1981). The language legislation has also been extensively tested in court, a process that is still not concluded. In 1984, the Canadian Supreme Court found part of Bill 101 to be unconstitutional on the basis of the new Constitution and Charter of Rights that resulted from the 1982 constitutional repatriation mentioned above. The Constitution stipulated that children with at least one parent who attened school in Canada have the right to attend the school of their choice (Kahn, 1985:123).

Conclusion

The defeat of the 1980 sovereignty-association referendum and the economic stagnation of the 1980s have deflected the tide of Quebecois nationalism to a considerable extent, but no one foresees a return to the state of affairs that existed in the past. Important steps have been taken by the Quebecois in gaining control over their own institutions, and this is likely to continue under future administrations. Clearly, their innovations require serious study by minority groups in other countries who are concerned about their culture, political, and economic status in relation to a dominant national group.

In the next section, I will explore the types of solutions that have come out of a very different structural setting, that of the People's Republic of China.

CHINA

The second case study presents a dramatic contrast with that of Canada. In place of an industrialized, capitalist, Western country, we have a relatively nonindustrial, socialist, Asian country. What they have in common is the necessity to deal with the problems posed by ethnic relations. The solutions that have resulted are very different.

Background

The Chinese currently officially recognize some fifty-five national minorities. The smallest of these groups number only a few hundred. The largest group, the Chuang, (or Zhuang), number over 13 million. Altogether, the minority groups constitute some 67 million people, or approximately 7 percent of the population of the People's Republic of China. Some of the more important minorities are the Mongols, the Tibetans, the Manchus, the Koreans, the Yi, the Miao, the Hui (Chinese Moslems), and the Turkish peoples of the northwest, of which the Uighur are the largest.

The majority national group within China are referred to as the Han, and they comprise the remaining 94 percent of the population. The Han, who had their origin in the Yellow River area, have been expanding outward for more than two thousand years, absorbing other national groups in the process. Although the Han are not themselves culturally homogeneous, a major unifying element is their use of the written Chinese language (Moseley, 1966a:14).

The way in which these groups are defined and thought of within China provides an interesting comparison with other areas. The nationality groups in China are not based primarily on racial characteristics (Eberhard, 1982:3–4). The Han are themselves a very heterogeneous group physically, as might be expected from their expansionist history. National distinctions are based largely on cultural characteristics, such as language, customs, religion, and economic way of life. The Hui are classified as a national minority almost exclusively on the basis of their Moslem religion, since in language and other cultural characteristics, they are like the Han. Although the Han have generally considered themselves more culturally advanced than the other groups with which they have come in contact, a racial ideology comparable to that of the West, which considers other groups biologically inferior, has not developed. Historically, the Han have been willing to assimilate other groups and consider as Han those people who have taken on the Han culture.

Thus, the national minority groups within China are groups that have been designated as a people based on a common culture and a common origin. However, these groups are by no means all equally distinct from the Han. A number of them, such as the Manchus, have been largely assimilated to Han culture. Others, particularly those who live in remote areas of China, remain very distinct in virtually all aspects (Moseley, 1966a:9–14; Deal, 1971:47).

The national minorities represent only six percent of China's population, and they are concentrated in many areas that are sparsely settled. As a result, they occupy over half of China's territory. Giving them added importance is the fact that many of their territories are border areas, and China's borders are very sensitive politically. The Mongols and Turkish people are located in the northwest, along China's border with Mongolia and the Soviet Union. The Tibetans border on India and the Himalayan states. The Chuang and other groups are located in southern China along the frontier with Southeast Asia. The question of national minorities in China, therefore, has had a political importance out of proportion to their numbers in the population.

The current distribution and characteristics of minorities in China is the product of a long historical process. From the time of the Ch'in dynasty (221–205 B.C.) to that of the Manchu dynasty (A.D. 1644–1911), China was ruled by a series of dynasties, many of which successively added to the territory of the empire. The prevailing belief during this long Imperial period was that the Han occupied the center of civilization. Outside the empire's core territory lay the vassal kingdoms, which paid tribute to the emperor and were generally governed by local rulers. Beyond the tribute kingdoms lay China's frontier areas, inhabited by what the Chinese considered to be barbarians. The Chinese were ethnocentric in that they believed that any non-Han could be civilized only by adopting the Han culture. Imperial China's frontier areas have today become Communist China's border areas inhabited by its many national minorities, many of whom have inherited a centuries-old suspicion of the Han based on the Imperial experience.

In 1911, China entered its Republic era when the Manchu dynasty was overthrown in a nationalist revolution led by Sun Yat-sen. The Republic of China, led first by Sun Yat-sen and then by Chiang Kai-shek, lasted until the Communists came to power in 1949. During this time, shifts in the official policy toward the minorities occurred. At times, they were promised national self-determination, by which was meant the right to self-government. At other times, this right was denied and a centralist policy proclaimed. Most of the time, the Nationalist position was that the minorities' assimilation of Chinese culture standards would be beneficial in that it would promote the unity of China. Whatever the position, however, the Nationalists' tenuous control of much of China made it difficult for them to implement their policies in a thorough or consistent manner.

It was during the period of the Republic of China that the Chinese Communists first came into contact with the national minorities. There was some contact with minority groups in the southwest in the 1920s, and specific reference was made to the rights of minorities in the Kiangsi Soviet Constitution proclaimed by the Communist party in 1931. The Long March (1934–1935), in which Communist armies covered over six thousand miles in fleeing from Nationalist troops, traversed extensive minority areas. Relations with the minorities during the Long March were varied. In some areas, the Communists were simply perceived as "Chinese" and resisted; in other areas, they had few difficulties and were even able to gain some minority recruits. Contact with the minorities continued during the period of resistance to the Japanese invasion, from 1937 to 1945. Thus, the involvement of the Communists with the national minorities predates the success of the revolution in 1949.

The Policy of Regional Autonomy

Prior to 1935, the position of the Chinese Communist party (CCP) with regard to minorities was modeled on that of the Soviet Union. This policy was based on the national minorities' right to self-determination, up to and including the right to secede and form a separate nation-state. The assumption during the 1920s and early 1930s was that a socialist China would be based on a federal union of republics with each of the major nationalities constituting a republic (Moseley, 1973:4). After 1935, when Mao Tse-tung rose to leadership position in the party, the policy shifted away from an emphasis on self-determination to an emphasis on building a strong and unified multinational socialist state. According to Mao's perspective, the necessity for unity in the face of foreign imperialism precluded the possibility of a right to secede.

With the seizure of power, it became necessary for the new government of the People's Republic of China (PRC) to make concrete their policy toward national minorities. The first major statement of this policy is contained in the Common Program of the Chinese People's Political Consultative Conference (1949), which was the initial basis for government policy in the PRC. Articles 50 through 53 deal explicitly with the national minorities (*The Important Documents* 1955).

Article 50. All nationalities within the boundaries of the People's Republic of China are equal. They shall establish unity and mutual aid among themselves, and shall oppose imperialism and their own public enemies, so that the People's Republic of China will become a big fraternal and cooperative family composed of all nationalities. Great nation chauvinism shall be opposed. Acts involving discrimination, oppression, and splitting of the unity of the various nationalities shall be prohibited.

Article 51. Regional autonomy shall be exercised in areas where national minorities are concentrated, and various kinds of autonomy organizations of the different nationalities shall be set up according to the size of the respective populations and regions. In places where different national minorities live together and in the autonomous areas of the national minorities, the different nationalities shall each have an appropriate number of representatives in the local organs of political power.

Article 52. All national minorities within the boundaries of the People's Republic of China shall have the right to join the People's Liberation Army and to organize local people's security forces in accordance with the unified military system of the state.

Article 53. All national minorities shall have freedom to develop their dialects and languages, to preserve or reform their traditions, customs, and religious beliefs. The People's Government shall assist the masses of the people of all national minorities to develop their political, economic, cultural, and educational construction work (ibid.).

In 1953, an official government statement was published entitled the "General Program of the People's Republic of China for the Implementation of Regional Autonomy for Nationalities." Article 2 states:

Each national autonomous region is an integral part of the territory of the People's Republic of China. The autonomous organ of each national autonomous region is a local government led by the people's government of the next higher level, under the unified leadership of the Central People's Government ("General Program," 1953:1–13).

Articles 4 and 5 provide for various types of autonomous regions, as where two national minorities jointly occupy an area, or where there is one large minority and several smaller ones. Article 12 reads:

People's governments shall be composed mainly of members of the national minorities concerned with the participation of an appropriate number of members from other national minorities and the Chinese inhabiting the same region (ibid.).

Article 20 states:

Free development of the economy is to be in accordance with the unified economic system and plan for economic construction of the state.

Article 23 makes clear that regulations drawn up by the autonomous governmental bodies must be approved by higher governmental bodies before becoming law.

Article 31 reads:

People's governments of higher levels shall make adequate appraisals of the special characteristics and actual conditions of each national autonomous region so that their directives and orders will conform both to the general line in the Common Program of the Chinese People's Political Consultative Conference and to these special characteristics and actual conditions.

Articles 32 through 34 state that the governments of higher levels will assist the autonomous regions in training minority cadres and in their political, economic, cultural, and educational development.

Article 40 reads:

The right of interpretation and of amendment of the General Program rests with the Central People's Government (ibid.).

The Constitution of the People's Republic of China, adopted in 1954, reiterates the same basic points:

All nationalities of our country are united in one great family of free and equal nations. This unity of China's nationalities will continue to gain in strength, founded as it is on evergrowing friendship and mutual aid among themselves, and on the struggle against imperialism, against public enemies of the people within the nationalities, and against both dominant-nation chauvinism and local nationalism. In the course of economic and cultural development, the state will concern itself with the needs of the different nationalities, and, in the matter of socialist transformation, pay full attention to the special characteristics in the development of each.

The People's Republic of China is a unified, multinational state.

All the nationalities are equal. Discrimination against, or oppression of, any nationality and acts that undermine the unity of the nationalities are prohibited.

All the nationalities have freedom to use and foster the growth of their spoken and written languages, and to preserve or reform their own customs or ways.

Regional Autonomy applies in areas entirely or largely inhabited by national minorities. National autonomous areas are inalienable parts of the People's Republic of China (*Documents of the First Session*, 1955).

These three documents set forth the key elements in the official minorities policy of the PRC. The major structural feature for the implementation of these policies lay in the system of regional autonomy, and this is the feature that attracted the most comment from outside observers.

The autonomous units that were set up as an outcome of this policy are organized at three different levels. The largest possible unit is the Autonomous Region, which is equivalent to a province. At this level are organized the Inner Mongolian Autonomous Region, the Sinkaing Uighur Autonomous Region, the Tibetan Autonomous Region, the Kwangsi Chuang Autonomous Region, and the Ninghsia Hui Autonomous Region. The next lowest level at which an autonomous unit can be organized is the Chou, or prefecture, which typically includes several counties. The smallest possible autonomous unit is the Hsien, which is equivalent to a county. The existence of different levels makes it possible to have autonomous governmental units where a minority is not large enough to warrant an entire autonomous region. It also makes it possible to have, for example, an autonomous Hsien for a small minority within an autonomous region established for a larger minority.

In addition to the regional autonomy structure, there are several central governmental and party organs established for dealing with minorities. The highest governmental administrative organ for this purpose is the Nationalities Affairs Committee of the National People's Congress, which serves to give representation to national minorities but has no real policy-making voice. The overall guiding policy for national minorities is set through the United Front Work Department of the party's Central Committee (Dreyer, 1972:416–17; Schwarz, 1963:151).

Chang Chih-i, a deputy director of the United Front Work Department, attempted in a 1956 document to spell out the specific functions of the autonomous area. According to him,

[t]he organs of self-government in national autonomous areas not only exercise the functions of a local element, identical with others, in the national administration but may also, under the authority granted by law and the Constitution: regulate the local budget; establish in accordance with the military law of the land, local security forces; and formulate autonomous regulations and independent laws that take into account the political, economic, and cultural peculiarities of the local people (Chang Chih-i in Moseley, 1966a:82).

The Implementation of the National Minority Policies

For purposes of discussing implementation it is possible to use the two dimensions of equality and community that were described in earlier chapters.

In this context, equality refers to efforts on the part of the Chinese to eliminate discrimination and oppression of the minority peoples who have historically suffered at the hands of outsiders, including the Han. It also refers to concrete measures taken to raise the standard of living of the minority nationalities, most of whom are worse off than the Han.

The official statements of the party and government in China constantly warn against the dangers of Han or Great Nation Chauvinism in dealing with the minorities, and stress that discrimination must be stamped out. Although there is a recognition that Han workers in the minority areas have not always lived up to this ideal, there does seem to be a sustained, well-publicized effort to eliminate oppressive practices and attitudes (ibid., Chapter 8). Chinese efforts to improve the situation of the minorities has not stopped with attitudinal changes. One practice instituted in minority areas after the revolution was to alter the terms of trade of goods produced in those areas in order to benefit the minorities (Moseley, 1973:135; Dreyer, 1976:115). In many cases, the central government has had to provide subsidies to the autonomous regions in order to stimulate their economies. In the case of the Xinjiang Uighur Autonomous Region (AR), for example, a recent study noted that

Xinjiang not only kept all local revenues for its own use, but also got huge subsidies from the central authorities. From 1955 through 1974, these central subsidies accounted for as much as 53 percent of Xinjiang's total revenue. State investments in Xingiang's capital construction in 1974 alone . . . were more than five times the 1955 total. Undoubtedly, the degree of economic growth and modernization in Xinjiang was in a large measure due to the enormous amount of state assistance provided to the region after 1949 (McMillen, 1979:290).

Literacy and general-educational campaigns were launched in areas where most needed, apparently with good success, and written languages were developed for those groups that did not have them (Schwarz, 1962:170–82; Dreyer, 1976:117). Several National Minority institutes have been developed to address themselves to the special schooling needs of the minorities. Other special provisions for national minority schooling have been made, including financial subsidies, priority in admission to regular schools, relaxation of age limits, and the establishment of schools in remote areas (Nichols, 1968:176–77). Health-care efforts have also been greatly stepped up in the minority areas. In Yunnan, for example, an area where malaria was prevalent prior to the revolution, the incidence of the disease had fallen to 1 percent of the population by 1956 (Moseley, 1973:110). Included here are the policy of regional autonomy, measures designed to preserve the minority cultures, and the practice of taking the minorities' "special characteristics" into account in implementing government policies. In all of these cases, it is clear that a tension exists between the socialists commitment to treat everyone equally and uniformly in building socialism and the practical necessity of acknowledging the existence of the different nationalities. This tension is apparent even in the original official policy-statements on the treatment of nationalities. The Chinese term for autonomous, *tzu-chih*, literally means "self-governing" (Schwarz, 1963:5). Yet the General Program clearly states that the autonomous governments are local governments under the direct control of higher levels of government. It also states that economic development in the autonomous areas shall be in accordance with the economic plans established by the central government. Likewises, the Common Program and the Constitution grant minorities the freedom to develop their languages but state ambiguously that they have the freedom to preserve *or reform* their traditional customs. The Common Program and the Constitution also provide for taking the special characteristics of minorities into account in formulating and implementing policies in their areas. Yet it is also clear from these documents that those policies must be in accord with the overall direction of Chinese national policy.

In order to get a clearer picture of how this problem of community has been dealt with, it is necessary to review the way the policies have been put into practice over time. An examination of the evidence indicates that some aspects of these policies have been fairly constant, while others have varied with changing national trends.

One constant feature has been the subordination of the autonomous areas to the central governmental and party organs with respect to the initiation of significant policy direction. Chang Chih-i restates the official position clearly when he states, "All national regional autonomous areas are parts of the Chinese People's Republic and cannot be separated from it; national regional autonomy is a local autonomy exercised under the unified leadership of the central people's government, and the organs of nationalities autonomy have the status of local government, depending on superior, national organs for leadership" (Chang Chih-i in Moseley, 1966a:81–82). Moseley notes that "the published reports concerning the establishment of autonomous areas in Kwangsi seldom reveal the tight control exercised by the state bureaucracy over the entire movement. Occasionally, however, the almost hidden force of the Party and Government reveals itself giving logical cohesion to a process which has the appearance of developing spontaneously" (Moseley, 1973:63). According to Moseley, the considerable local participation involved in the adoption of many policies in the autonomous areas is "induced participation" (ibid., 65). Ultimately, it seems that the party is the key factor in maintaining central control. Schurmann describes the organization of party control in the following passage:

It is hierarchically organized, which means that the whole structure resembles a pyramid. It has a far-flung base ramifying throughout the society in alter-ego fashion alongside every organized unit of state and society. Wherever there is a factory, bureau, school, production brigade, military company, there also is a unit of the Communist Party. This parallelism makes it possible for the party to exercise direct leadership over every unit of organization to which it is linked. Linkage is created by the fact that leaders of the organizational unit arer members of the Party and thus subject to Party discipline (Schurmann, 1968:139).

In this connection, it should be noted that the party, unlike the government, is not organized along the lines of regional autonomy, and the top party positions are monopolized by Han (Lee, 1973:195ff; McMillen, 1979:230, 292–93; Connor, 1984:540).

Minority control of the regional autonomy areas has also been diluted by PRC policies of gerrymandering and Han colonization. This thesis on gerrymandering has been developed in a recent analysis by Walker Connor that is largely unsympathetic to the PRC. He argues that the Han political elite distrusted the minorities' political loyalty after the revolution, and that this distrust was expressed in part by drawing the boundaries of the autonomous regions in order to maximize central government control. In the cases of Inner Mongolia and the Kwangsi Chuang AR, this took the form of making the designated ethnic groups minorities within their own autonomous regions. In the case of Tibet, where Tibetans were the overwhelming majority, it took the form of leaving a significant number of Tibetans outside the boundaries of the AR (Connor, 1984:323ff; see also Lee, 1973:156ff).

Connor and others have also emphasized the impact of Han migration, or "colonization," on the autonomous regions. Han migration into the minority areas was encouraged by the government after the revolution, and has continued since then. The policy apparently served multiple purposes, including the economic development of those areas, an outlet for overpopulated Han areas in central China, and the political integration of the ARs with the rest of China (McMillen, 1979:10, 65; Connor, 1984:327–29; Schwarz, 1963:540). Although exact population figures are not available, it appears that the combined impact of gerrymandering and colonization had resulted by the 1970s and 1980s in a situation in which the Chuang were about one-third of the Kwangsi Chuang AR; the Uighurs were about 45 percent of the Sinkiang Uighur AR, with other minorities about 20 percent; the Hui were approximately one-third of the Ningsia Hui AR; the Mongols constituted only some 10 to 20 percent of the Inner Mongolian AR; and the Tibetans may have been down to about half of the Tibetan AR (Dreyer, 1972:437; McMillen, 1979:10; Nichols, 1977b:7; Connor, 1984:323–28).

A counterbalancing factor has been the attempt by the PRC to expand the number of minority cadres in the governing bodies of the autonomous units. Data indicate a steady growth in the proportion of minority cadre to Han cadre in these areas, but also considerable unevenness from region to region. In Mongolia, for example, it is relatively high, whereas in Tibet, it is relatively low, apparently as a result of historical factors (see Nichols, 1977a, 1977b; Dreyer, 1972:417).

At the time of the success of the Liberation movement, few cadres were in the minority areas, since the revolution had been carried out essentially by the Han with the marginal participation of the minorities. Since it was felt that socialist reform would be more readily accepted by the minorities if it was carried out by their own people, Mao Tse-tung put a great deal of emphasis on the recruitment and training of minority cadres after 1949. Cadres were enrolled in special training institutes charged with the task of instilling the political and technical skills necessary for the implementation of socialist reform in the minority areas. A particular effort was made to recruit intellectuals. The minority cadres, as the crucial link between the minorities and the central authorities, often found themselves in a delicate position. On the one hand, some of the cadres have been considered sell-outs and lackeys of the Han by their own people, particularly since they have been charged with carrying out policies that might have inspired local resistance (Dreyer, 1972:437–38). This not only created grave personal problems for them but lowered their ability to carry out their assigned tasks. On the other hand, minority cadres who identified closely with their minority group could come under criticism for being nationalists and for subverting the work of building socialism. At times, conflict occurred among the minority cadres and locally assigned Han cadres (Nichols, 1968:11). At certain points in time, particularly during mass campaigns such as the Cultural Revolution, criticisms of the minority cadres as undoing the work of the revolution led to significant numbers of them being purged.

In addition to the relatively constant factors mentioned above are a number of other aspects of nationalities policy that have been subjected to considerable variation depending on the prevailing political currents. One of these is the policy toward the traditional elites in minority areas, often referred to as the upper level personages. The traditional elite are those persons in minority areas who enjoyed special influence prior to the coming of socialism by virtue of their economic, religious, or political positions. The Communists, on taking power, faced the problem of how to deal with these persons, whose personal interests did not coincide with the building of socialism. While acknowledging the existence of class contradictions between the upper level personages and the minority workers, the CCP leadership recognized that the traditional elite continued to have considerable local influence. Thus, it was decided to operate on the basis of the United Front with the elites, granting them certain concessions while at the same time encouraging the work of socialist reform that would eventually undermine their position (Chang Chih-i in Moseley, 1966a:130–31). This moderate and long-term strategy received some criticism during the period of the antirightist campaign and the Great Leap Forward (1957–1960), but it continued in operation until the mid-1960s. During the Cultural Revolution, however, which began in 1965, a broad attack was launched on the strategy of the United Front and on the traditional elites. The main focus of the attack on the elites was their continued active opposition to the work of the revolution and their oppression of the workers in their areas. The new emphasis was on speeding up the work of socialist reform in the minority areas and eliminating any special consessions to members of the old elites (Dreyer, 1972:443–47).

The attitude taken toward the so-called special characteristics of the minorities and their role in policy formulation and implementation parallels the experience of the traditional elites. The underlying consideration in both cases had to do with the extent to which the distinctiveness of the minorities was acknowledged. The special characteristics policy had been invoked whenever it was considered necessary to modify a general policy in its application to a minority. Thus, land reform and the establishment of cooperatives had been delayed in some minority areas because it was felt that their rapid imposition would lead to disruption and increased resistance to central authority. This policy underwent severe modifications starting in 1957. The antirightist campaign started in that year took the form in the minorities areas of an attack on local nationalism, and the invocation of the principle of special characteristics was seen as a manifestation of nationalism and a slowing down of the pace of socialist transformation (Moseley, 1973:123). It was now argued that unless all the nationalities advanced together, dangerous disparities would be perpetuated in China and the unity of the country would be threatened. The new emphasis on socialization at the expense of special characteristics was reinforced by the cooperative and commune movements and the Great Leap Forward from 1957 to 1960. However, the attempt to produce rapid change in a uniform manner did, in fact, create widespread social disorganization in the minority areas. This was manifested in some areas in lowered agricultural production. In Tibet, it was manifested in a revolt in 1959. The generally disappointing results of the new policy and the waning of the Great Leap Forward led to renewed respect for the special characteristics of the minority areas after 1960 (Moseley, 1965:8). With the coming of the Cultural Revolution in 1965, however, special characteristics policy incurred another attack, and a demand was made that all the citizens of China be treated on the basis of class rather than nationality. Thus, the tension between uniformity and distinctiveness has continued to manifest itself in this policy area as in others.

One final aspect of nationalities policy that needs to be examined is that having to do with the preservation or reform of minority cultures. As noted above, the official documents are ambiguous in that they speak of preserving *or* reforming the minorities' cultures. The writings of Chang Chih-i are important in this regard, since they seem to represent an attempt to spell out some more-concrete guidelines for dealing with this question. At the time he wrote this, Chang was a deputy director of the United Front Work Department of the CCP. According to him,

[t]he traditional customs and habits of the national minorities can, for the most part, be divided into three categories. We should, in accordance with the spirit of the Constitution and on the basis of the free will of the masses of the national minorities, adopt different attitudes with respect to the three groups. (1) We should promote and make use of those which are favorable to development and production. . . . (2) As for those which are not injurious to, or which influence only slightly, the production and development of the nationality, or which may have had some influence on physical health but whose influence on present production is not too great, then their desires in the matter should be complied with or the right moment to advance their education awaited. . . . (3) The national minorities must, as conditions permit, be taught constantly to abandon customs that are harmful to their development and to the present requirements of production (Chang Chih-i in Moseley, 1966a:117-18).

Chang thus attempts to differentiate the policy toward aspects of the minority cultures, depending on the extent to which they conform or fail to conform to overall national-policy goals and to the general requirements of socialism. This, however, represents the short-term policy. In another section of this work, Chang devotes some attention to long-run considerations:

Reciprocal amalgamation between nationalities . . . is an existing phenomenon. The more that different nationalities come into contact, the more they influence one another, especially when one of the nationalities is comparatively advanced in government, economy, and culture and therefore in a position to influence heavily the more backward nationality. Over a long period of time, this mutual influence will lead to the gradual disappearance of the original differences between them. This kind of natural assimilation is an unavoidable and progressive phenomenon as well as a natural law. We are opposed, however, to an assimilationist policy. The more a policy of oppression and assimilation is employed, the more fearful are the minority nationalities of losing their identity and the more a spirit of fierce resistance is produced among them; only by letting them base the development of their political, economic, and cultural life on their own special characteristics can the ways of life of each of the nationalities be brought closer together and improved; in this way, they can more easily be induced to cast off their backwardness. This is appropriately dialectical (ibid., 36–37).

Several interesting points emerge from this concise statement. In speaking of "reciprocal amalgamation," Chang is using a concept that appears to be closely related to the Anglo-U.S. concept of the melting pot. However, he candidly admits that the preponderant direction of influence will be toward the "more advanced" nationality, i.e., the Han. When one adds to this the consideration that the Han are an overwhelming majority, and rapidly increasing their numbers in the minority areas through migration, it is clear that the key concept here is that of "natural assimilation." The chief difference between this policy and that which Chang characterizes as just plain "assimilationism" is that it relies less on coercion and more on sociological processes, or "natural laws," operating in the long-run. The end result, that is, "the gradual disappearance of the original differences," appears to be the same, since the more advanced nationality cannot be expected to take on the characteristics of the less advanced (see also Lee, 1973:277ff).

While the general principles operating in this policy area appear to be those stated by Chang, it is also true that these policies have fluctuated over time in response to national political currents. Policies aimed at the minority languages illustrate this point. In the early years of the PRC, there was considerable emphasis on developing writing systems for the minority languages that had none, on promoting the use of the minority languages in the schools, and on publishing works in the minority languages (Schwarz, 1962:170–82). Starting around 1958, however, during the Great Leap Forward and related movements, a shift toward a deemphasis on creating writing systems for the minority languages took place, and Chinese became required for the minority students in all grades of primary school (Hung-mao Tien, 1974:4; Lee, 1973:282ff). This line was softened somewhat after the period of the Great Leap Forward, but the Cultural Revolution appears to have produced a renewed deemphasis on the minority languages. Since the Cultural Revolution, a swing back toward the use and development of those languages, and toward having cadres learn the languages of the areas in which they are working, has developed. The fluctuations in language policy that have taken place reflect essentially tactical shifts. The main underlying consideration does not appear to be cultural preservation as an end in itself. Rather, the major guiding considerations have been two: (1) the recognition that written languages and literacy were important for economic development in the minority areas (Schwarz, 1962:172) and (2) the desire to increase literacy rapidly in order to facilitate political socialization and the transmitting of policy directives from the center to the frontiers (Hung-mao Tien, 1974:3).

One traditional socialist expression that is frequently invoked in the question of cultural preservation is that of "national in form and socialist in content." The basic idea is to use traditional cultural forms in art, song, dance, and literature, but to inject them with socialist content in order to promote political education and identification with the PRC. The following anonymous song is an illustration of "national in form, socialist in content":

The Hearts of the T'ais Come Closer to the Sun

Listen! my T'ai brethren,
The Kun-lo Highway is now completed.
Like a blood vein,
It links the frontier closely with the heart of the motherland,
Enables the T'ais' hearts to come closer to the sun (*Union Research Service*, 1963:352–53).

From this brief review, it can be seen that the implementation of the national minority-policies in China has been a complex process involving the interaction of several distinct factors. Furthermore, it has fluctuated over time in response to broad political currents. The main stages in the implementation process have been the following:

(1) an initial stage, lasting from 1949 to about 1956, in which regional autonomy was established and considerable attention was given to the special characteristics of the minorities;

(2) a second period from 1957 to 1961 during which the emphasis was

on socialist reform in the minority areas and fewer concessions were made to distinctiveness;

(3) a period from 1962 to 1965 that represented a kind of halfway point or compromise between the two earlier periods;

(4) the period of the Cultural Revolution, 1965 to 1968, with a renewed emphasis on reform and renewed attacks on local nationalism; and

(5) the current period, from 1969 to the present, during which there has been a relaxation of pressure on the national minorities, and in which minority cultures have been allowed greater scope again (Moseley, 1965:16–18; Hung-mao Tien, 1974:1–3; Dreyer, 1976:262ff).

However, recognition of these various phases should not obscure the fact that fundamental continuities and underlying principles in the formulation and implementation of the national minority policies have existed. There have also been persisting tensions, particularly with regard to the "community" dimension. One of the key factors here has been the level of urgency associated with the class struggle within China. Clearly, it has been felt by the CCP leadership that making too many allowances for the minority areas would slow down or possibly reverse the desired process of social transformation. The traditional elites, if given too much leeway, would give first consideration to their own class interests. True regional autonomy might play into the hands of these elites. The minority cadres might fall under the spell of local nationalism and be coopted by the local elites, rather than waging a vigorous class struggle. In addition, the traditional cultures are seen as generally reinforcing social patterns of a nonprogressive nature. Thus, it is not surprising that the attitude toward minority distinctiveness has fluctuated with the priority assigned to the class struggle.

It is also important to reemphasize the fact that the eventual, long-term goal has remained quite constant, and that policy fluctuations represent tactical differences among contending Han factions rather than fundamentally divergent goals. This is a point on which virtually all of the major studies on Chinese national minorities policy agree.

Walker Connor notes the 1980 publication in all of China's major newspapers of a posthumous Chou En-lai speech, in which he states, among other things:

The Han are so numerous simply because they have assimilated other nationalities. . . . Assimilation is a reactionary thing if it means one nation destroying another by force. It is a progressive act if it means natural merger of nations advancing toward prosperity. . . . The Huis are so huge in number just because they have succeeded in absorbing people from other nationalities. To absorb and expand—what's wrong with that? (cited in Connor, 1984:428).

Connor goes to say that "the posthumous publication of Chou En-lai's speech was therefore a reminder that, while the CCP had returned to a policy of national flourishing, assimilation remained the ultimate goal of the party." (ibid.).

Roots and Determinants of the Minorities Policy

The underlying determinants of the Chinese national minorities policy can be grouped under five general headings: (1) the socialist roots, (2) the dimension of economic development, (3) the dimension of national security and national integration, (4) the class struggle, and (5) continuities with traditional Han concepts and practices.

In the Chinese writings on the subject, frequent reference is made to socialist antecedents on "the national question," particularly to the works of Lenin and Stalin. Stalin is primarily cited for his definition of a nation, which reads in its summary form: "A nation is a historically constituted stable community of people, formed on the basis of a common language, territory, economic life, and psychological makeup manifested in a common culture" (Shaheen, 1956:42). However, this definition has not been rigidly adhered to by the Chinese in defining their national minorities. The Chinese practice has been that of a broad definition of a national minority.

Lenin, of course, was the real theoretician on the national question in the Soviet Union, as Stalin himself acknowledges through his frequent references to Lenin's contributions. Several of his themes have entered into the Chinese formulation. The key to Lenin's discussion lies in his concept of the right to self-determination, by which he means fundamentally the right of the national minorities to secede and form their own state(s) (Lenin, 1968:47).

According to Lenin, each minority must have this right and must be able to make the decision to secede on its own. Lenin justified the right of self-determination on several grounds. At the most general level, he argues that this right is in keeping with the spirit of democracy and should be adhered to by socialists, who are by necessity democrats (ibid., 7–9). More specifically, Lenin felt that granting the right to secede was the only effective means for guaranteeing that the minorities would not be oppressed by the majority (ibid., 74). Another justification was that recognizing the right to self-determination was the best means for eliminating national resentments on the part of the minorities, and that this would thus accelerate the development of class consciousness among the workers of all nationalities, who might otherwise become fixated on national jealousies (ibid., 169). Lenin was fond of quoting Marx to the effect that no nation that oppresses another nation can itself be free.

As noted above, the original position of the Chinese Communist Party was based on the acceptance of the right of national self-determination. Although this position changed after Mao achieved leadership of the party, the Chinese retained Lenin's emphasis on giving special attention to the situation of the oppressed nationalities. The specific form this took was regional autonomy, an idea that had also been endorsed by Lenin and Stalin (Stalin, 1942:52ff; Shaheen, 1956:78–79).

Another aspect of Lenin's position was the heavy stress he laid on the equality of nations and on combating great-nation or oppressor-nation chauvinism, and this carried over more directly into Chinese practice. Although recognizing the potential danger to international worker solidarity posed by minority nationalism, Lenin felt that a graver threat was posed by chauvinistic attitudes on the part of the majority. Particularly in the years immediately following the revolution, Chinese propaganda reflected this emphasis.

The Chinese attitude toward the assimilation of minorities also has important socialist roots, as can be illustrated in the writings of Lenin. Lenin argued for the desirability of an international culture of democracy and of the world working-class movement, purified of all elements of the bourgeois culture that was dominant in capitalist societies. Although Lenin claimed that such an international working-class culture was not nonnational in form—and

therefore not uniform in terms of language, customs, and so on—
it seems clear that the basis thrust of his analysis is assimilationist.
Lenin writes of "capitalism's world-historical tendency to break down
national barriers, obliterate national distinctions, and to *assimilate*
nations—a tendency which . . . is one of the greatest driving forces
transforming capitalism into socialism" (Lenin, 1968:21; emphasis
in original). In another section, Lenin states, "The proletariat cannot support any consecration of nationalism; on the contrary, it
supports everything that helps to obliterate national distinctions
and remove national barriers; it supports everything that makes
the ties between nationalities closer and closer, or tends to merge
nations" (ibid., 28). In its Chinese version, this attitude has taken
the form of support for the fusion of nationalities within China, a
process to be followed eventually by the disappearance of nationalities throughout the world (Moseley, 1965:22). The preference
for a noncoercive "natural assimilation" is anticipated in Lenin's
statement that the proletariat "welcomes every kind of assimilation
of nations, except that which is founded on force or privilege" (Lenin,
1968:28).

Although the socialist tradition of thought on the national question had its impact on the Chinese policy, an even greater influence was exerted by two broad policy goals, each linked to the
situation of China at the time of the Liberation. One of these goals
was rapid economic development. China at the time of the revolution was an underdeveloped country with a history of dependence or semidependence on the more industrialized countries.
Rapid economic development was important in maintaining the
loyalty of the people of the regime, in insuring the autonomy of
the Chinese state, and in building toward a socialist society. Yet
many of the minority areas were less developed economically than
the Han areas, and it was difficult to formulate and apply economic
policies in a uniform manner. The policy of regional autonomy allowed for a more differentiated treatment. Economic development
policies could be fully applied in the Han areas, which were already more developed and more firmly under central government
control. At the same time, special allowances could be made for
the minority areas, based on their special characteristics, without
impeding the economic process in other parts of China. The national minorities could be allowed to make the transition to social-

ism at a slower pace. Of course, this practice has been subject to fluctuations, as described above, particularly when rapid social change has been stressed.

The other major policy goal, not unrelated to the first, was the achieving of national integration and national security. When the Socialists came to power, many of the border areas were only nominally under the control of the Chinese state, e.g., Tibet and Sinkiang. This state of affairs threatened the territorial integrity of China and presented a grave danger of infiltration by hostile foreign states, particularly the capitalist countries. The traditional distrust of the Han on the part of the frontier peoples added to this danger. Elements of the defeated Kuomintang armies remained in bordering countries to the south and were receiving support from the United States. The Sino-Soviet split also created threats on the northern borders of China.

By setting up governmental bodies in which the minorities had special representation and by making allowances for special characteristics, it was hoped that the minorities could be won over to the PRC. The goals of security and integration would thus be advanced. It was apparently felt that a hard-line policy of uniformity would increase minority resistance and fuel local nationalism. The location of the national minorities on China's sensitive frontiers has been an important factor in the formulation of policies affecting them.

A fourth source of Chinese policies toward minorities has been the attitude toward the class struggle. Specific allowances for the national minorities have been adopted when they have been seen as compatible with the ultimate goal of socialist transformation. At such times as policymakers have decided that the requirements of such transformation have changed, the policies toward national minorities have changed accordingly. The specific nature of these changes was described in the preceding section.

The overall impact of these considerations, of course, has led to significant departures from the recommendations of other Socialists, particularly Lenin. These departures, and the policy of regional autonomy in particular have been justified as "the practical result of the Chinese Communist Party's application of Marxist-Leninist theory on the national question to the facts of the Chinese revolution" (Chang Chih-i in Moseley, 1966a:80). It is argued that self-determination is not desired by the minorities, and that at any rate, it is unnecessary because they are already liberated.

There is a fifth determinant of the national minorities policy, one that is intriguing but difficult to evaluate. This has to do with the continuities of prerevolutionary Han Chinese attitudes and practices. One of these traditional attitudes is Han ethnocentrism and paternalism toward the non-Han. This takes the form among Han Socialists of regarding themselves as "elder brothers" to the minorities, who must assist the minorities in overcoming their backward ways and attaining the high cultural level of the Han (see, for example, Chang Chih-i in Moseley, 1966a:75, Chapter 4; see also Deal, 1971:41). The traditional Han feeling of superiority is enhanced by the perception that they carried out the revolution with little help from the minorities, and that the Han are thus once more leading the way to a higher stage of social, political, and cultural development. Han paternalism comes through even in those statements that warn against Han chauvinism.

Another traditional attitude and practice that shows continuity under socialism is that of assimilating the non-Han into Han culture and society. The Han have traditionally accepted into Han culture any group that takes on their ways. This practice, which has been in effect for two thousand years, shows no sign of diminishing under socialism.

However, one of the factors that makes it difficult to evaluate the independent effect of these Han traditions on current policy is that they are reinforced by elements of socialist tradition. Socialist writers in general are as ethnocentric as the Han in their assumption that there are higher cultures and lower cultures and that the lower ones must advance to the level of the higher ones. In the West, this has taken the form of a pronounced Europocentric view in relation to the Third World, found in the writings of Marx and Engels as well as Lenin and others (Avineri, 1969). In China, it manifests itself in the attitudes toward the national minorities and other Asian nations as well. With regard to assimilation, the quotations cited above from Lenin are illustrative of the profoundly assimilationist stance of socialism. Neither in the case of the Han nor among socialists in general is there a regard for cultural diversity as a desirable end in itself.

The difficulties of disengaging certain traditional Han attitudes from socialist tradition does not allow us to establish the specific effect of either in these particular policies. All we can say is that in these respects, they reinforce each other, and together exert a powerful influence on the policies toward national minorities.

CONCLUSION

In this chapter, I have examined two very different societies and how they have handled the question of ethnic relations in order to see what useful things might be learned from their experiences. It is clear that neither of them can serve as an ideal "model" of ethnic relations, and yet there are positive elements in both experiences.

Several limitations can be readily seen in the case of Canada. Obviously, the English-speaking majority do not favor cultural pluralism, and it is only a historical accident that conditions conducive to minority control of a provincial government exist there. (It should also be noted that the Francophones in Quebec are not particularly eager to advance the cultural autonomy of other minorities in that province.) Also, important national constitutional limitations on provincial autonomy exist in Canada, although those limitations are not quite as strict as they are in the United States. It is also true that economic inequality persists in Canada between the major ethnic groups, although the Francophones are not disadvantaged to the same degree as blacks or Chicanos in the United States.

On the other hand, the Quebecois do have a significant degree of institutional and territorial control, and they have used it to implement important legislation designed to safeguard their culture and to improve their economic position. Much of that legislation has centered on language rights.

In the case of China, we have a situation where the government officially recognizes the national minorities and sets up areas of regional autonomy of various sizes in acknowledgment of their special status. However, the degree of "autonomy" exercised by these areas is strictly limited, and in most of them, the titular minority group is not a majority within its own autonomous area. The majority Han policymakers see cultural pluralism as a temporary situation, one that will "wither away" as the society approximates the communist ideal in the future. It is also the case that a high degree of Han paternalism toward the minority groups continues to exist.

On the other hand, minority rights are recognized to a significant degree, and for the present, minority cultures are encouraged and even subsidized. Allowances are made for the special characteristics of the minority nationalities, and the government does make serious efforts to curb Han ethnic chauvinism. Economic policies with respect to the autonomous areas are designed to raise the standard of living there. The existence of socialism removes the motivation for large private employers to exploit and manipulate minority workers, a process that has been a major factor in perpetuating racism and discrimination in U.S. history (see my *Race and Class in the Southwest,* 1979).

Thus, although neither Canada nor China should be adopted uncritically as a model of ethnic relations, both provide positive elements for the construction of such a model. In the next chapter, we will look to Switzerland and Nicaragua to provide additional insights.

8

Learning from Experience, Part II: Switzerland and Nicaragua

In the previous chapter, we consideed two countries that differ considerably from each other but that have each worked out an ethnic accommodation based on a degree of limited regional territorial control by their minorities. In this chapter, we will examine two more countries that differ markedly from each other as well as from Canada and China. Yet here, too, we will see systems that have sought to achieve a more equitable relationship among their ethnic groups through arrangements of regional control. In the case of Switzerland, such a system has deep roots, extending back to prefeudal times. In the case of Nicaragua, the "social contract" between the major groups is still in the process of being worked out. Small as these two countries are, each has a great deal to interest its larger neighbors.

SWITZERLAND

Located in the very heart of Europe, Switzerland borders on France, Germany, Austria, and Italy. Historically buffeted by the political currents from each of those countries, Switzerland has maintained a position of international neutrality since the sixteenth century. It is famous for its traditions of participatory democracy and for its remarkable degree of political decentralization, as well as for the "ethnic peace" that exists among its major constituent groups. As we shall see, all of these patterns are interrelated in complex and subtle ways.

Background

Switzerland is a confederation, or federal union, of twenty-three cantons, three of which are divided into half-cantons that essentially function as cantons. The original Swiss Confederation was formed in 1513 on the basis of thirteen cantons. Over the years, others have been added, with the most recent, the Jura, being carved out of the canton of Bern in 1979.

In 1970, the official population of Switzerland was 6.3 million, of which 75 percent were German-speaking, 20 percent French-speaking, 4 percent Italian-speaking, and 1 percent spoke a Latin-derived language known as Romansch. Approximately 55 percent of the population is Protestant, and 43 percent Catholic (Schmid, 1981:16). French is the official language of four of the cantons (Geneva, Vaud, Neuchâtel, and Jura); Italian is the official language of one (Ticino); three cantons are bilingual, German and French (Bern, Fribourg, and Valais); one is trilingual, German, Italian, and Romansch (Graubünden, also known as the Grisons); all the rest are officially German-speaking (Zürich, Lucern, Uri, Schwyz, Unterwalden, Glarus, Zug, Solothurn, Basel, Schaffhausen, Appenzell, St. Gallen, Aargau, and Thurgau) (Schmid, 1981:20).

Modern-day Switzerland is a relatively wealthy and industrialized country, with large urban centers such as Zurich, Basel, Geneva, Bern, and Lausanne. Less than 10 percent of its inhabitants are currently employed in agriculture. The leading economic sectors are machinery and metalworking, chemicals, watches, textiles, food processing, banking, and insurance. Short on natural resources, except for water power, Switzerland specialized at an early stage in producing high-quality manufactured goods. The chemical industry arose largely out of the production of dyes for textiles, and the machine industry out of the watches and textile sectors. Swiss neutrality and political stability have drawn funds from abroad to its banking and insurance sectors (Thurer, 1970:168–73). Growth and prosperity since World War II have attracted a large number of foreign workers, who have become an important social and political issue in recent years.

Switzerland's political system is complicated and unique. The national executive is the Federal Council (Bundesrat), which is composed of seven members who are elected by parliament to four-year terms. One of the seven serves as president, but the office is for only one year and rotates among the members. Each of the seven councillors serves as head of an administrative department. By an informal understanding, the members are chosen from the four major political parties: two from the Catholic Conservatives (Christian Democratic Part, or CVP); two from the Liberals (Free Democratic Party, or FDP); two from the Socialists (Social Democrats, or SPS); and one from the Peasants Party (Swiss People's party, or SVP). This is known as the Magic Formula. Also by custom, at least two of the councillors are non-German. Regional and religious balance is also provided for in the selection of members (Schmid, 1981:36; Steinberg, 1976:82ff; Girod, 1974:208–11; Steiner, 1974:17–34; Hughes, 1975:132ff).

The Swiss national parliament is composed of two chambers. The National Council (Nationalrat) is elected directly by the people through a system of proportional representation. The small Council of States (Standerat) consists of two representatives from each canton and one from each half-canton. Thus, the Swiss national assembly is similar in concept to that of the United States, reflecting the federal nature of the two systems. In Switzerland, however, political power is much more decentralized, although that has been changing as the country industrializes.

The twenty-six cantons and half-cantons exercise a great deal of authority, and each has its own unique constitution and its own set of political institutions, including a cantonal parliament. They retain all rights that are not expressly delegated to the national government. Each of the cantons also has its own variation on the party system, and the national parties are generally like federations of the cantonal parties (Steinberg, 1976:80). The regulation of language and other cultural matters is largely left to the canton.

The situation is made even more intricate by the existence and importance of the Swiss communes, the units of local government, which have their roots in the structure of Germanic tribes existing even before feudalism (Barber, 1974:Chapter 5).

The basic unit of Swiss politics, and the key to understanding them, is the Gemeinde or commune. There is no suitable English translation of Gemeinde because there was no parallel development in the English-speaking world. The nearest equivalent is, perhaps, the self-governing New England town, where the citizenry assembled in the town meeting constitute the ultimate legislative authority. In certain parts of Switzerland from earliest times . . . the community of free citizens has always been understood as the lawful "sovereign," and in Swiss political parlance today, the citizenry as a whole is still the "sovereign." . . . Typically there is no "Swiss citizenship" as such. A Swiss person is in the first place a citizen of his Gemeinde and as such a citizen of his canton and hence automatically a Swiss citizen. In theory each of the 3,072 Gemeinden in Switzerland could draw up its own regulations for conferring citizenship. In practice communal citizenship must meet certain requirements set by the cantons which in turn have to meet national legal stipulations. There is, as befits anything Swiss, great variety in spite of cantonal supervision in the provisions governing citizenship of a Gemeinde or commune (Steinberg, 1976:57).

The communes have been one of the vehicles for the Swiss tradition of direct democracy, but not the only one. Several of the mountain cantons continue the practice of the Landsgemeinde, the assembly of all free citizens in a large open space for the purpose of considering legislation. In some cantons, the Landsgemeinde dates back to the thirteenth century (ibid., 1976:73–74).

Switzerland also makes extensive use of the referendum and initiative for the direct expression of citizen political preferences. In the initiative, either at the cantonal or national level, a law can be proposed by gathering a certain number of signatures. It has the effect of a recommendation to the appropriate parliamentary body. The referendum is used to get popular approval for national or cantonal constitutional changes and can also be used to challenge legislative acts (Hughes, 1975:128–31; Steinberg, 1976:74ff).

The intricacy and attention to detail that characterize political life in Switzerland make it resemble one of their own fine watches. Some of the flavor of the system is conveyed by the British historian Jonathan Steinberg in the following passage:

The existence of separate cantons with separate institutions makes Swiss politics and social life fundamentally different from that of a centralised state. Cantonal identity, like the powers of the Gemeinden, provides a receptacle for differences. It is the foundation of Swiss multilingual, religious and social peace. Each canton resembles a set of Chinese boxes or, perhaps, a beehive, into which history has built dozens of smaller boxes, the Gemeinden, or communes. They in turn are often subdivided into ethnic, religious or cultural sub-units which, while not formally recognized, give the commune its characteristic colour or tone. This cellular political system allows ethnic and other particularisms to flourish side by side. It gives to Swiss political life a marvelous mosaic surface (Steinberg, 1976:64).

An Abbreviated Swiss Chronology

The history of Switzerland as a political unit is generally traced to the year 1291, when three Alpine valley communities signed a treaty in order to maximize their independence from the Habsburg lords of the Holy Roman Empire. The three communities, now cantons in central Switzerland, were Uri, Unterwalden, and Schwyz (from which the country takes its name). These mountain valley communities, the "Talgenossenschafter," were communally organized associations of largely free peasants. During the next two centuries in the general region, a complex set of alliances emerged of towns and rural communities in opposition to the attempts of European feudal aristocracies to control the fragmented area. The two major alliances were those of Switzerland (or Helvetia) and of neighboring Raetia, now the canton of Graubünden. Their military prowess eventually made the Swiss a major European power during the fifteenth and early sixteenth centuries, essentially free from external control.

In 1513, the Swiss Confederation was formed with thirteen cantons, all German-speaking with the partial exception of Fribourg, where French was also spoken. The confederation survived the next two centuries, although severly strained by religious wars between Catholic and Protestant and by the intrigues of the European great powers. During this period, the confederation remained an alliance of sovereign states, with little central administration.

In 1798, Switzerland was invaded by France. After briefly imposing a unitary republic, the French reestablished the Swiss Confederation, adding six new cantons out of areas that had been allied and subject territories (St. Gallen, Aargau, Graubünden, Thurgau, Ticino, and Vaud) (Thurer, 1970:91).

After the downfall of Napoleon and the defeat of France, the Congress of Vienna in 1815 redrew the map of Europe, and Switzerland essentially assumed its modern boundaries. Geneva, Valais, and Neuchâtel were added as cantons, and the predominantly French-speaking and Catholic Jura region was added to the largely Protestant and German-speaking canton of Bern in a move that was to have long-term political repercussions (see below). The Federal Pact that created the new system provided for a weak central government, and reaffirmed Swiss neutrality.

During much of the rest of the century, Switzerland was wracked by conflicts between Catholics and Protestants and between liberals and conservatives. In 1830, the July revolution in France set into motion a liberal and anticlerical political surge in Switzerland, and resulted in a number of modernizing and egalitarian reforms (Thurer, 1970:102; Martin, 1971:215ff). In 1845, the Sonderbund War pitted a separatist confederation of seven Catholic cantons (Lucerne, Uri, Schwyz, Zug, Unterwalden, Fribourg, Valais) against the rest of Switzerland in a conflict that involved a number of overlapping issues, including the role of the Catholic church, the degree of centralization of the Swiss state, and a general liberal-conservative dimension (Martin, 1971:220ff; Thurer, 1970:106ff).

The defeat of the Sonderbund alliance resulted in the 1848 Constitution, which, as revised in 1874, remains the basic Swiss Constitution of today and which transformed the confederation into a modern federal state. It established the Council of States and the National Council, mandated universal male suffrage, and stipulated that German, French, and Italian would be the three official languages with equal legal status. Religious conflict continued in the 1860s and the 1870s, however, in the "Kulterkampf" struggle. Constitutional revisions in 1874 banned the Jesuits and strengthened the central state apparatus.

Switzerland remained neutral during World War II, although German nationalism had some appeal within its borders. At the end of the war in 1918, a dramatic General Strike paralyzed the country. Although the strike was over quickly, its political impact was considerable. It resulted in a shortening of the work week and an expansion of the welfare state, as well as in a system of proportional representation for electing the National Council that greatly strengthened the underrepresented Social Democrats (Steinberg, 1976:41–44; Thurer, 1970:147–48).

In 1937, a labor agreement was signed between the metalworkeres and the machine industry that largely replaced the strike with outside arbitration. It eventually spread to other sectors of the economy. So effective was it in maintaining industrial peace that only three major strikes occurred in the entire country between 1973 and 1974 (Ziegler, 1979:84).

Switzerland also managed to stay out of World War II, and in the postwar decades, entered an extended economic boom, which has resulted in material prosperity but which has also transformed the country in ways that challenge the traditional localism and decentralization of the system. It also brought in a large number of foreign workers, a phenomenon that has caused strains for the traditional concept of Swiss national identity.

Another challenge to tradition took place in 1971, when Swiss women were finally given political rights at the national level by passage of a referendum. There is irony in the fact that a country that prides itself on its democratic traditions took so long to grant women suffrage.

In 1974, another series of referenda began, which resulted in 1979 in the Jura district of Bern becoming the country's twenty-third canton.

Ethnic Accommodation

Switzerland is an unusual country in many ways, not least of which is the remarkable ethnic accommodation it has reached among its major ethnic groups. It is important to recognize that this accommodation is not idiosyncratic but is instead closely related to other aspects of Swiss society and intimately bound up with Swiss history. It is one part of a larger picture.

A major aspect of that pattern, as has been indicated earlier, is the historical emphasis on decentralization to the level of cantons and communes. Swiss society has been largely built from the bottom up. Indeed, it was not until the nineteenth century that one could really say that a national Swiss state existed, with the national institutions one usually associates with such a state (a central

legislative and executive power, a national army, and so on). In
the process of state consolidation, however, a large degree of decentralization was retained. This pattern made it possible to avoid
major ethnic conflicts at the national level by leaving a great deal
of discretion to the cantons, which usually have a specific ethnic
identity. Although there are bicultural and even tricultural cantons, each major group has "its" cantons, which form a strong cultural base.

That is only one part of the big picture, however. There is also
a deep-seated cultural preference in Switzerland for arriving at decisions on the basis of amicable agreement, or consensus, rather
than by strict majority rule or power conflict (Steiner, 1974:chapters
1, 2). The agreements reached in the labor-management field since
1937 are one example, as in the so-called Magic Formula used in
the selection of Federal Council members. It is also possible to see
the recognition of the three major languages as official languages
with equal rights as part of this cultural pattern.

James Dunn summarizes the relevant cultural patterns in the
following passage:

(1) The existence of the canton as the basic unit of decision and action.

(2) The existence of a consensus-seeking style of decision-making. This
is not surprising for local communes and the smaller rural cantons, but
it seems to have been present in most of the city cantons also.

(3) If consensus could not be achieved, and if a conflict proved to be so
intense that the decision of the cantonal majority was totally unaccept-
able to the minority, and if the two groups occupied more or less
distinct geographical areas, then the solution was to split the canton.

(4) At the confederal level, respect for cantonal rights demanded that
each canton be treated as an equal. This afforded a powerful degree of
protection for important minorities, especially religious and linguistic
ones.

(5) Because of the tradition of cantonal consensus, and the consequent
political and social homogeneity of the cantons, the really emotional
conflicts tend to be displaced to the level of the confederation, where
some sort of modus vivendi is eventually reached. Thus the cantons
become buffers between the citizen and these dangerous conflicts. They
permit him to remain attached to his particularisms at the cantonal
level, while reducing the tension in the country as a whole. This, of

course, implies that there is no irresistible pressure from a central government which may be controlled by a group in opposition to the one which controls the canton. Thus:

(6) resistance against all efforts to increase the scope of the confederation's authority and to centralize decision-making in its hands. This resistance has been especially strong in those cantons most likely to be put in a minority by a more centralized regime—i.e., Catholic, and French- and Italian-speaking cantons (Dunn, 1972:17).

One important aspect of the Swiss ethnic accommodation is the relative economic parity that exists among the three major language groups. In 1975, the French-speaking Swiss represented about 20 percent of the population and earned about 23 percent of the national income (19,297 Swiss francs compared to the national average of 19,036) (Schmid, 1981:34). The canton of Ticino, where the bulk of the Italian population is concentrated, ranked fifteenth out of twenty-five cantons and half-cantons in the 1975 income figures, with an average per capita income of 15,910 Swiss francs, or 84 percent of the national average. German-speaking cantons ranged from among the wealthiest to the poorest (ibid., 35).

A second aspect has to do with the degree of political representation of the linguistic minorities. As mentioned above, at least two of the seven members of the Federal Council are French- or Italian-speaking.

Similar conventions for representation of the diversity of language and religion also apply to parliamentary committees, the judiciary, the public service, and federally supported corporations. For example, even the small Italian-speaking group, which comprises only 4 percent of all Swiss citizens, is overrepresented in the civil service, with 7.6 percent of all federal administrative employees, 6.0 percent of postal employees, and 11.9 percent of railway employees. Only at the upper levels of the administrative grade of the civil service is the proportion of Ticinesi and Italian Swiss from the Grisons [Graubünden] precisely equivalent to their numbers in the population (ibid., 39–40).

Another very important aspect of ethnic accommodation has to do with cultural policies, particularly those dealing with language and education. The tradition of respecting linguistic rights in Switzerland is longstanding, and is tied to the general emphasis placed on localism in Swiss history (Warburton, 1976:91). The 1798 Constitution of the short-lived Helvetic Republic contained the provision that German, French, and Italian would have equal rights, and that arrangement has been perpetuated ever since (McRae, 1964:6–7).

The legal equality of those three languages is recognized in a number of ways in the workings of Swiss federal institutions. All federal laws are published in all three languages, and members of parliament may speak in any of the three (ibid., 23ff). In its dealings with the public-at-large, the federal government must adapt to the language of the individual where the three official languages are concerned. This is known as the principle of personality (Personalitatsprinzip). All personnel in the federal government's central administration are required to be bilingual, and sometimes trilingual. The Federal Tribunal, the highest federal court, is required by the Constitution to have representatives of all three official languages. Military regulations are also made available in all three languages, and officers are expected to be bilingual or trilingual. Government support for radio and television broadcasting is distributed in such a way as to insure coverage in the three major languages (ibid., 42ff).

The federal government since 1931 has also made grants to the cantons of Ticino and Graubünden for the support of Italian and for Romansch, which has been designated since 1938 as a "national" although not "official" language (Schmid, 1981:24).

The general aim is to protect and strengthen the cultural and linguistic heritage of the region, and this includes support of a wide range of activities, including conferences, courses on language and literature, encouragement of writers and artists, aid for local theatrical and musical groups, grants to libraries and museums, protection of historic monuments and architecture, and subsidies for publication (McRae, 1964:53).

The contrast with the cultural suppression and assimilationist practices of countries like the United States could hardly be more striking.

In accordance with Swiss federalism, all linguistic matters not explicitly delegated to the central government remain within the jurisdiction of the cantons. In accordance with the "principle of territoriality" (Territorialprinzip), "any canton or linguistic area has the right to preserve and defend its own linguistic character against all outside forces that tend to alter or endanger it" (McRae, 1964:11). Cantons have official languages, just as the central government has. As noted earlier, most of the cantons are unilingual, three are bilingual, and one is trilingual. Even in the multilingual cantons, however, there are clearly defined language areas for the most part, and the principle of territoriality is extended down to the level of the commune. Only six of the more than three thousand Swiss communes have changed their dominant language since 1848 (ibid., 13).

The official language of the canton is the only language in which cantonal laws must be published and is the language of instruction in the schools. Immigrants who move from one language area to another are expected to assimilate linguistically to their new home, and this is seen as an important guarantee that each language group will be able to safeguard its territorial linguistic base (ibid., 12).

The school system is basically the responsibility of the canton, and education is carried on in the official cantonal language. In a few bilingual areas, a dual school system is maintained to accommodate both language groups. (ibid., 37). Instruction in a second language usually begins in the sixth or seventh school year and is required at the secondary level (Schmid, 1981:48; McRae, 1964:37). A recent study indicated that 65 percent of German Swiss had a working knowledge of French and 52 percent of French Swiss had a knowledge of German (Schmid, 1981:30). All seven Swiss universities are under cantonal control. Instruction in three of them is in German, while another three offer instruction in French. One is bilingual French and German, but there are currently no Italian universities (McRae, 1964:41).

Kenneth McRae summarizes the prevailing attitude toward language in Switzerland in the following passage:

Recent Swiss history has been a period of rapid social change, and new problems have arisen continuously to disturb traditional relationships between the language groups. To find solutions—even imperfect solutions—consonant with the principle of linguistic equality has demanded unremitting effort and sometimes constitutional innovation of a highly imaginative kind. In modern Switzerland this effort has been willingly made, and the fact may be worthy of reflection in other plurilingual countries where it is customary to take either a fatalistic or a majoritarian attitude towards the pattern of language usage (ibid., 72).

The Jura

A closer examination of the Jura region casts further light on the nature and workings of the Swiss ethnic accommodation, since it is the part of the country that has seen the most ethnic conflict.

From the tenth to the eighteenth century the Jura was a principality ruled by the prince-bishop of Basel. This bishopric was a part of the Holy Roman Empire of the German nation. The Congress of Vienna in 1815 added it to the Swiss canton of Bern in the general rearrangement of European boundaries that took place after the defeat of Napoleon. Bern is a predominantly German and Protestant canton. The Jura is made up of seven districts, six of which are Francophone and one German-speaking. The three northern francophone districts are largely Catholic, while the three southern ones are predominantly Protestant.

From the beginning, this "shotgun wedding" was marked by tension, although less so in the southern districts, which shared a religious orientation with the rest of Bern and which had been allied militarily with Bern while still under the Holy Roman Empire (Mayer, 1968:721). A number of the tensions revolved around the religious conflicts that affected all of Switzerland in the nineteenth century. The Kulturkampf struggle of the 1860s and 1870s between the Swiss state and the Catholic Church left a legacy of bitterness in the area.

The language issue was a point of contention at first, but the 1830 cantonal constitution recognized French as an official language, a status that was reaffirmed in the 1846 constitution (ibid., 725–27). In a further concession to Jura demands, it became the practice after 1846 to reserve two of the nine seats on the cantonal executive council for Jurassian representatives. This practice was made official by amendments to the constitution in 1950 (ibid., 727, 733).

During the twentieth century, the religious conflict died down, as it did in the rest of the country. However, the sense of estrangement on the part of many Jurassians apparently continued, and in the late 1940s, a surge of sentiment developed for separation from the canton of Bern. The spark occurred in 1947, when a Jurassian was passed over for an important cantonal government post in favor of a German-speaker. Out of the ensuring agitation emerged the "Rassemblement jurassien," which pushed for the formation of a new canton and was self-consciously nationalistic. In 1959, an initiative designed to lead toward that end was put to a vote, and resulted in the three northern Francophone Jura districts voting yes, with the other four (three French-speaking and one German-speaking) voting no (ibid., 736). Although the total Jura vote was negative, the separatist agitation continued to grow. In the early 1960s, a militant youth wing of the Rassemblement jurassien was formed, and from 1962 to 1964, another separatist organization called the Front de liberation jurassienne carried out a number of terrorist attacks (Steinberg, 1976:67; Mayer, 1968:739). Antiseparatists formed their own organizations in the southern Jura districts, and the situation appeared to become more and more polarized.

A resolution to the Jura problem was finally achieved through a series of complex referendums beginning in 1970 on the initiative of the Bern cantonal government. A 1974 referendum in the Jura alone resulted in a vote of 36,802 for the creation of a Jura canton, and 34,507 against (Steinberg, 1976:69). In 1975, in the follow-up referendum, the three southern, Protestant, francophone districts decided to stay in the canton of Bern. The one German-speaking district (Laufen), voted to incorporate itself into another adjoining canton (Schmid, 1981:131). Finally, in 1978, a countrywide referendum approved amending the Swiss Constitution to create a new canton of Jura out of the three northern districts that had voted for separation. It came into existence in 1979 as the twenty-third canton.

Varying interpretations have been put forth to explain the case of the Jura, which appears so different from other regions of Switzerland. Kurt Mayer stresses the conjunction of linguistic and religious factors in producing a sense of alienation on the part of the northern Jurassians (Mayer, 1968:737–38). In a comparative study of four Swiss cantons, William Keech points out that there are other regions that have dual minorities but in which there is no comparable conflict. He concludes that the history of grievances plays a key role in the Jura, dating back to the original forced incorporation of the area into the canton of Bern (Keech, 1972:402–3). But perhaps the most striking thing about the conflict is not that it existed, but that the Swiss were able to resolve it in a democratic manner despite the long history of bitterness and antagonism that had characterized it.

The Gastarbeiter

Although the Swiss have worked out an ethnic accommodation marked by a great deal of mutual respect and toleration, it is not universal in its scope. It is, rather, a "bounded" accommodation among its historic constituent groups, as can be seen through an examination of the position of foreign workers, or Gastarbeiter.

Foreign or "guest" workers have been a widespread phenomenon in Western Europe in the postwar years, nowhere more so than in Switzerland. The demand for labor from the booming economy led to the importation of ever greater numbers of foreign workers in the 1950s and 1960s, so that by the early 1970s, they accounted for about one-fifth of all employees, and 37 percent of all industrial workers (Steinberg, 1976:90–92). They were concentrated in certain industries, particularly building, machines and foundries, textiles, and hotels and restaurants (Hughes, 1975:213).

The various categories of foreign workers consisted of (1) those with permanent resident status (310,000 in 1974); (2) those with a renewable annual visa (289,000); (3) seasonal workers (saisonniers), whose visas allowed them to remain in the country for shorter periods (152,000); and (4) frontier crossers, who lived in other countries and commuted daily to work in Switzerland (111,000) (Steinberg, 1976:91). In order to achieve resident status, a foreign worker had to be in Switzerland for ten years (Schmid, 1981:143). Only after twelve years could one apply for citizenship, a status that the Swiss grant very grudgingly.

In 1974, the major countries of origin of the foreign workers were as follows (Steinberg, 1976):

Italy	41%
Spain	20
France	11

| Yugoslavia | 8 |
| Germany | 7 |

By 1978, the proportion of Italians had increased to almost half of the total (Schmid, 1981:140).

The increasing number of foreigners in Switzerland eventually led to a backlash, particularly as the composition of guest workers shifted toward southern and eastern Europe. In 1970, a publisher and member of the national legislature, James Schwarzenbach, sponsored an initiative to limit the number of foreign workers to no more than 10 percent of the population of any given canton. Despite opposition from all leading economic and political organizations in the country, the initiative received a 46 percent yes vote (Steinberg, 1976:92–93). Other initiatives sponsored by antiforeigner groups in 1974 and 1977, proposing even more extreme limitations, received declining percentages of positive votes (Schmid, 1981:145).

Some interpretations of these reactions have focused on Swiss workers' fears of economic competition and Protestants' fears of eventual Catholic domination. However, Bernard Barber has noted that the greatest support for the Schwarzenbach initiative came from several pastoral, Catholic, inner-Switzerland cantons, and he has suggested that the support was ultimately based on a more general feeling that the old, familiar Switzerland was rapidly being swept away by the forces of modernization.

The telling distribution of votes lends credence to a different interpretation of the Schwarzenbach affair that, while it does not deny nationalist and racist attitudes, suggests the primacy of a more basic socioeconomic and value struggle in the contest. In its simplest terms, it suggests that the opponents of Schwarzenbach were not merely tolerant liberals defending the international civil rights of hard-working foreigners, but were the combined forces of efficiency, national planning, centralization and economic progress representing the political and industrial elite of the Swiss nation. And it suggests that his supporters were not simply bigoted reactionaries, but advocates of an integral communal past founded on autonomous self-government (Barber, 1974:225).

Conclusion

A number of varying interpretations have been given for the relative success of the Swiss ethnic-accommodation. One of the most common interpretations focuses on the existence of what are termed crosscutting cleavages. By this is meant that major potential lines of identification and conflict do not coincide and reinforce each other, but intersect. Particular stress is put on language and religion in this interpretation. Thus, it is noted that a substantial proportion of German-speakers are Catholic, and that many French-speakers are Protestant.

Another line of interpretation points out that Swiss neutrality reduces the burden of problems with which the state must deal and allows greater energy and attention to be devoted to resolving internal problems.

Other factors that are mentioned frequently are the relatively stable demographic proportions that have prevailed in Switzerland for some time—so that no ethnic group feels it is about to be overwhelmed by another—and the nonmajoritarian attitude on the part of the German-speaking group (Schmid, 1981:151). The fact that French, German, and Italian are all well-known languages with substantial international prestige is also seen as contributing to attitudes of mutual respect.

The general tradition of decentralization and localism clearly contributes as well, in that it makes it possible for each major group to exert considerable cultural and political control over its historic territorial base.

Notwithstanding whatever weight is given to these various factors, it nevertheless seems clear that Switzerland comes closer to an "ethnic model" than either of the two cases examined previously: Canada, where the Quebecois have had to surmount considerable opposition to attain the limited provincial control they now enjoy, and where economic inequality is still an issue between Francophones and Anglophones; and China, where efforts at achieving greater material equality among the ethnic groups are tempered by what remains a long-term assimilationist attitude on the part of the Han majority. The Swiss have thus come closer to achieving a balanced solution that takes into account both equality and community, although, as we have seen, equal rights are not readily extended to groups that are not part of the historic Swiss constituency.

In our final case study, we will turn to a country where ethnic relations are compounded by racial complications, something that has not entered into our analysis as a major factor up to this point.

NICARAGUA

Nicaragua is a relatively poor country of less than three million inhabitants, located in the heart of Central America. The bulk of the population is mestizo, a mixture of Native American and European stock, and is concentrated in the western half of the country, or the Pacific Coast. The eastern half of the country is referred to as the Atlantic Coast, and it is here that the bulk of the ethnic and racial minorities are concentrated.

The Pacific Coast includes over 90 percent of Nicaragua's population and contains most of the major cities, such as Managua, Granada, Leon, Masaya, Esteli, and Matagalpa. The economy of the region is almost entirely dependent on such pastoral and agricultural products as cotton, cattle, coffee, and various food crops. Although there are still communities in western Nicaragua that maintain an Indian identity, the cultural differences between them and the majority group are subtle. The Indian groups in this part of the country all use Spanish as their normal language (Dunbar Ortiz, 1984:191–92).

The Atlantic Coast is much less populated than the Pacific Coast, as one might expect from its rain-forest ecology. It was estimated to contain approximately 280,000 people in 1981, or about 10 percent of Nicaragua's population (CIDCA, 1982:49). Historically, little connection has existed between the two sections of the country, a condition the present government is trying to change through its campaign of national integration.

The major ethnic groups on the Atlantic Coast are as follows, based on a demographic study by CIDCA, the Nicaraguan government's main research organization in that part of the country:

(1) *Mestizo,* 182,000, representing 65 percent of the population on the Atlantic Coast. Although mestizos have been represented on the Atlantic Coast since the last century, their present numerical dominance in this

area is of relatively recent origin. Starting in the 1950s, the pace of mestizo in-migration accelerated as small farmers from the Pacific Coast were increasingly displaced from the land by the growth of larger agricultural holdings (ibid., 45). They have concentrated in the southern and south-central parts of the Atlantic Coast region, where they have set up small farms.

(2) *Miskitu* (also spelled Miskito), 70,000, or 24 percent. The Miskitus are the largest of the Native American groups in Nicaragua. The total Miskitu community in Central America is divided by the border between Nicaragua and Honduras, and is estimated to number some 120,000 (Dunbar Ortiz, 1984:259). The Miskitus are concentrated in the northeastern part of the region, where they constitute a local majority. They speak their own native language, although many also know Spanish and/or English. The number of Miskitus has been on the increase for the last three centuries, contrary to the experience of most Native American groups (ibid., 217). They have been in contact with Europeans for several hundred years now, and their culture has been significantly shaped by that contact. There has also been considerable racial mixture with African slaves who came to the area via Caribbean islands. From the seventeenth to the nineteenth century, the Miskitus acted as intermediaries for the British through a form of indirect colonialism on the Atlantic Coast, and their expansion demographically and geographically stems in large part from that status. That process took place at the exense of other Native American groups in the area (Hale, 1983:19-22; Dunbar Ortiz, 1984:202ff).

(3) *Creole*, 26,000, or 9 percent. The Creoles are racially mixed but predominantly African in origin, being the descendants of slaves brought to the Atlantic Coast and to Caribbean islands by English colonizers (CIDCA, 1982:33ff; "Los Afro-Nicaraguenses [creoles] y la Revolucion," 1986:7-8). They speak a Caribbean dialect of English and are located in the southern part of the Atlantic Coast. Their largest concentration is in the port of Bluefields, the largest town in the region, where they represent about 35 percent of the population (K. Yih, 1985:111).

(4) *Sumu*, 4,900, or 1.7 percent. This group of indigenous people is located in the northern part of the Atlantic region, away from the coast. They represent the remnants of several related Indian groups that suffered demographic decline after European incursions into the area. Part of their decline was a consequence of conflicts with the Miskitus, armed with British weapons, and part was a result of cultural assimilation to mestizos and Miskitus (CIDCA, 1982:23ff).

(5) *Garifuna*, also know as Black Caribs, 1500, or .5 percent. This group is descended from Africans and from Carib Indians from St. Vincent Is-

land: they speak the Carib language. Much larger concentrations of Garifunas are found in Honduras and Belize. Within Nicaragua, they live in small communities close to Pearl Lagoon, on the southern coast (CIDCA, 1982:39ff; Dunbar Ortiz, 1984:192).

(6) *Rama*, 600, or .2 percent. The Rama are a small remnant of what was at one time a much larger indigenous people. They are located only in a small area to the south of Bluefields (CIDCA, 1982:17ff).

There were also some merchants of Chinese descent on the north Atlantic Coast, but they apparently left the country after the triumph of the Sandinista revolution in 1979 (Bourgois, 1981:36). In general, the social stratification system in the region in the twentieth century has found the Native American groups at the bottom, with the Creoles having a larger middle class and representing a kind of intermediate stratum. There are few creoles in agricultural labor ("Los Afro-Nicaraguenses [creoles] y la Revolucion," 1986:12–13). Mestizos have occupied the top rungs, although in this very poor region, those rungs do not reach very far. Many of the displaced mestizo farmers who have moved into the area in recent decades, of course, are also very poor, so that mestizos are actually found at all of the occupational levels on the Atlantic Coast (K. Yih, 1985:112–13).

A Historical Outline

Prior to the sixteenth century, the area that is now Nicaragua was occupied by a variety of Native American peoples who spoke several different languages. Beginning in the 1520s, the area was colonized by Spain. The town of Granada was founded in 1524, and Leon soon thereafter. Spanish control of the Pacific zone soon had a devastating impact on the native peoples. Within a span of a few decades, an estimated half-million Indians were transported to gold-mining areas such as Peru and to Caribbean islands to work as slaves. An estimated additional half-million perished, as a result of war and disease, or left the area. By 1600, fewer than 10,000 indigenous people lived in the region, accounting for the relative absence of such groups to this day in western Nicaragua (Dunbar Ortiz, 1984:200–202).

The Atlantic Coast, on the other hand, was never effectively penetrated by the Spanish colonizers. What raids there were into that area did have the effect of striking fear into the Indian people, making them receptive to British overtures in the next century.

The British, operating from their base in the Caribbean, soon developed a relationship of indirect colonialism with the Atlantic Coast, and the Miskitus became their intermediaries (Bourgois, 1981:27). In 1687, the English created the position of King of the Mosquitia to rule as their agent in that region, with the king being named by the British governor of Jamaica. According to contemporary scholars, many of the kings of the Mosquitia were in fact Creoles, and the headquarters of the king was in Bluefields (Dunbar Ortiz, 1984:238; Yih and Slate, 1985:25). However, the king is remembered today as the Miskitu King.

In the eighteenth century, the Spanish authorities in Nicaragua stepped up their efforts to gain control of the Atlantic Coast, and in the latter part of the century, the British largely withdrew from the area (Bourgois, 1981:28). In 1821, the Central American Federation declared its independence from Spain, and in 1838, Nicaragua became an independent republic. At this time, the British renewed their ties with the Indians of the Atlantic Coast and sought to regain their influence in the region (Dunbar Ortiz, 1984:209). This move was countered by the United States, however, which sought to limit the power of European countries in the hemisphere and to increase its own control under the Monroe Doctrine.

By 1860, the U.S. had forced Britain to renounce formal sovereignty over the Mosquitia. The Treaty of Managua, which formalized the British withdrawal, created a "Mosquitia Reserve" on the Atlantic Coast. The reserve retained limited governmental autonomy, with an ambiguous political relationship to the Nicaraguan government. Territorial boundaries, for example, never were clearly defined, causing endless jurisdictional disputes. Despite these ambiguities, or perhaps because of them, U.S. companies had little trouble acquiring land concessions for their operations. By 1890, 90% of commerce on the coast and a good part of foreign investment was in U.S. hands. The earliest U.S. investment was in banana and lumber concerns located near the port town of Bluefields (Hale, 1983:23–24).

In 1894, the Atlantic Coast was occupied militarily by Nicaraguan forces in what came to be known as the reincorporation of the area. The king was deposed, and the Mosquitia was renamed the province of Zelaya.

The second half of the nineteenth century was marked by increasing U.S. economic penetration into the Atlantic Coast. Beginning in the 1880s, a number of lumber companies began operations there, exploiting the extensive mahogany, cedar, and pine forests (Jenkins Molieri, 1986:139ff). Their general practice was to clear-cut the forests in pursuit of quick profits and then to leave the area. Banana plantations were also established by such companies as United Fruit, Standard Fruit, Cuyamel Fruit, and Atlantic Fruit in the period from the 1890s to the 1930s. Many of these companies left Nicaragua in the 1930s as a result of a combination of factors, including soil depletion and attacks by the forces of Sandino.

Mining was another important extractive industry dominated by foreign companies. A variety of metals were extracted, particularly in the period from the 1930s to the 1970s, when most of the readily available reserves were exhausted (Dunbar Ortiz, 1984:215). Marine animals have been the most recent of the Atlantic Coast resources to be exploited by foreign, particularly American, companies. After World War II, the lobster, shrimp, and sea turtle industries showed significant development. The companies relied heavily on Miskitus as turtle hunters, but the yield soon declined as hunting proceeded in an unregulated manner. The approach of the companies is summed up by a North American geographer:

The investment philosophy for many foreign-owned companies, such as the turtle factories, is quick return on low investment and overhead and reinvestment elsewhere, when the market or resource fails. The turtle companies, for example, were fully aware that the [turtle] population would be decimated through intensive commercial exploitation. No matter, a healthy return would be realized on investment and the resultant ecological "costs" would be borne by others (Nietschmann, 1979:9).

Indeed, the common denominator of all of these economic activities was damage to the environment, a major legacy of the corrupt, U.S.-influenced governments that ruled Nicaragua prior to the 1979 revolution. Unfortunately, the environmental protections that have been put in place by the Sandinista government have become a source of tension with the Miskitus and other coastal people (Dunbar Ortiz, 1984:217).

U.S. political and military intervention closely paralleled the economic penetration of Nicaragua. In 1909, the marines landed in Bluefields in support of a Conservative revolt against the Liberal President Zelaya. Zelaya was overthrown, and a Conservative president was installed who was more receptive to U.S. wishes, particularly with respect to economic policies (Weber, 1981:6ff). The marines were to remain in Nicaragua, off and on, but mostly on, until 1934, during which period the United States virtually dictated Nicaraguan economic policies. It was this blatant American intervention that led to the organization of a resistance movement from 1928 to 1932, led by Augusto Sandino. The major targets of Sandino's forces were the U.S. Marines and such companies as Standard Fruit (Jenkins Molieri, 1986:90ff).

Never able to crush Sandino's nationalist revolt, the marines pulled out of Nicaragua in 1933. Before they left, however, they organized Nicaragua's National Guard, headed by Anastasio Somoza. In 1934, Somoza engineered the assassination of Sandino and shortly thereafter took over the government of Nicaragua. Thus began a more than forty-year period of rule by the Somoza family, with strong U.S. backing. Successive American administrations followed the dictum of President Franklin D. Roosevelt that Somoza was "a son-of-a-bitch, but our son-of-a-bitch." During this period, there was little organized resistance to rule by the Somozas, who gradually concentrated the country's economic resources in their own hands and those of their close followers. Before the overthrow of their dynasty, the Somozas had pursued such a rapacious course that they managed to alienate virtually all major sectors of Nicaraguan society. Surprisingly enough, one never heard voiced during this period the U.S. concern for Nicaraguan democracy that has been so much in evidence since the 1979 revolution.

In 1962, the Sandinista Front for National Liberation (FSLN) was founded by a handful of intellectuals and activists headed by Carlos Fonseca, setting in motion a protracted struggle that culminated in 1979 in the overthrow of the Somoza regime and the establishment of a new, revolutionary government enjoying broad popular support.

The new government launched major programs of economic development, land reform, literacy, and health improvement but was soon faced with a major counterrevolutionary movement organized and financed by the United States. Beginning in 1981 with the newly elected Reagan administration, the CIA recruited a Honduras-based force led by officers of Somoza's defeated National Guard, and set out to overthrow the new government of Nicaragua. Despite the pressures of war on its northern border conducted by these "contra" forces, Nicaragua held elections in 1984 for a National Assembly and a president. The election was contested by seven parties and resulted in the FSLN gaining majority control of the National Assembly and electing one of its top leaders, Daniel Ortega, to the presidency. On the Atlantic Coast, the FSLN received 70 percent of the vote in the northern district and 65 percent in the southern district. The three elected representatives from the coast to the National Assembly were all minorities and all affiliated with the FSLN (Butler, 1985b).

While all of this activity was taking place, predominantly in the Pacific Coast region, other events were occurring on the Atlantic Coast. A predominantly Miskitu organization had been founded in the 1970s entitled ALPROMISU (Alianza para el progreso del Miskitu y Sumu). It served as a general-purpose political advocacy organization, taking up such issues as land claims and formal Miskitu representation in the government of Nicaragua (Dennis, 1981:284–85; Adams, 1981:25; Jenkins Molieri, 1986:89). In November of 1979, shortly after the triumph of the revolution, Comandante Daniel Ortega addressed a large gathering of ALPROMISU activists on behalf of the Sandinista regime. At this meeting,

[h]e emphasized that the Miskito and Sumu should not think of themselves as Indians. They were among the poor, and they should identify with the poor of the world. The revolution was not made just for Indians but to help all the poor. Also, they should first identify themselves as Nicaraguans for the revolution was for all Nicaraguans, not just for Indians. Specifically, they should identify with the other *campesinos* [peasants, small farmers] of the world, and not with other Indians of the world. . . . Thus he sought to create a class and national identity, to cut across and discard the ethnic identification that lay clearly behind the ALPROMISU organization (Adams, 1981:25, 55).

Ortega's advisors were able to persuade him to accept the continued presence of an ethnically based organization, and ALPROMISU was subsequently transformed into MISURASATA, Miskito–

Sumu–Rama–Sandinista–Asla Takanka (united together). According to the anthropologist Richard Adams, the inclusion of the southern Nicaragua Rama in the organization indicated the initial confusion of the largely mestizo Sandinistas from the Pacific Coast when faced with questions of ethnic identity and organization on the Atlantic Coast (ibid., 55). MISURASATA was then granted a seat on the ruling council of the national government and was allowed to lead the literacy campaign in the Miskitu area, conducted in the Miskitu language (Dennis, 1981:286).

In 1980, demonstrations took place in Bluefields by Creoles, with complaints about the presence of Cuban health workers and teachers and demands for a stepped-up program of coast improvements (Dunbar Ortiz, 1984:249; Dennis, 1981:290). Consultations with representatives of the national government were apparently successful, and the southern Atlantic Coast has been comparatively peaceful since then.

During 1981, relations between the Miskitus and the Sandinista government deteriorated rapidly. For various reasons, which are described more fully below, considerable mutual distrust existed between the two groups. In the 1979–1981 period, MISURASATA leaders such as Steadman Fagoth repeatedly confronted the national authorities, using any concessions to add to their own support among their Miskitu constituency (Hale, 1983:55).

A turning point came in February of 1981, when government authorities arrested thirty-three MISURASATA leaders on the grounds that they were preparing a separatist movement and that they had ties to ex-Somoza and CIA operatives (Dunbar Ortiz, 1984:241; Hale, 1983:57). The government's unease had been triggered in part by MISURASATA's Plan '81, which claimed rights to a third of Nicaraguan territory for indigenous people (Jenkins Molieri, 1986:231ff). Four soldiers and four Miskitus were killed when resistance to the arrests broke out. Although all of those arrested were released shortly, the damage had been done. Several thousand young Miskitus crossed over into Honduras and joined efforts with contra forces, and during that same year, the best-known Miskitu leaders also joined the opposition to the Sandinistas. Among them were Brooklyn Rivera, Armstrong Wiggins, and Steadman Fagoth, who was charged by the government with having been an agent for Somoza prior to the revolution (Dunbar Ortiz, 1984:241).

During 1981, the Reagan administration also took on an increasingly belligerent pose toward Nicaragua. In December, U.S. President Ronald Reagan approved operations by the CIA against Nicaragua, and it was disclosed in congressional hearings that the CIA had already been providing support to contras based in Honduras (ibid., 250). Also during December a series of attacks were initiated by contras in the Rio Coco area, which marked the boundary between Nicaragua and Honduras and was an area of dense Miskitu settlement. According to Nicaraguan government sources, the attacks were part of a plan called Operation Red Christmas, led by Fagoth and others, designed to lead to a general Miskitu uprising. The existence of this U.S.-backed plan was confirmed during the 1987 U.S. congressional hearings into the Iran-contra scandal. As a result of the attacks, a state of military emergency was declared in the region. Although there was no uprising, another large number of Miskitus crossed into Honduras, where they were settled in refugee camps. As a result of the attacks, a state of military emergency was declared in the region by Nicaraguan authorities, and the remaining population along the Coco River was evacuated and moved to temporary quarters away from the border. This involved some eight thousand Miskitus (Hale, 1983:69; Dunbar Ortiz, 1984:252).

The events of 1981 seriously polarized the situation on the Atlantic Coast, and relations have remained tense since that time. However, there are some positive signs. In 1983, the Nicaraguan government announced unconditional amnesty for indigenous people who had been involved in counterrevolutionary activities and released most of those who were in prison at that time (Quesenberry and Dunbar Ortiz, 1986:2). In 1984, an official government commission was formed to formulate a plan for regional autonomy for the Atlantic Coast, and in the same year, a new organization named MISATAN was created among Miskitus to work within the revolutionary process. In 1985, the government began returning Miskitus from the temporary settlement camps to their home communities along the Rio Coco. That same year, a draft document on regional autonomy was circulated for comments. In addition, bilingual education programs have begun in Spanish–Miskito and in Spanish–English (Norwood and Zeledon, 1985; Yih and Slate, 1985).

Historic Factors Shaping Ethnic Relations

On taking power in 1979, the Sandinista government inherited a difficult situation with respect to the Atlantic Coast. Indeed, ethnic and race relations in Nicaragua were complicated by historic factors stretching back several centuries.

The first of these factors was the catastrophic effect that Spanish colonization had had on the indigenous population of Nicaragua and Central America in general. The Miskitus today still refer to mestizos from the Atlantic Coast as "the Spanish," (los españoles) associating them in this way with that whole history of exploitative relations. The alienation of the two coasts was compounded by British penetration of the Atlantic coast and by the anti-Spanish and then anti-Nicaraguan Republic alliance they forged with the Miskitus. The king the English established on the Coast came to symbolize Miskitu independence, and the "incorporation" of the area into Nicaragua is perceived in the collective memory as an imposition by the disliked "Spanish" (Dennis, 1981:281).

The presence of foreign, especially American, companies on the Atlantic Coast in the late nineteenth and early twentieth centuries, and Sandino's subsequent attacks on them, created additional difficulties.

Another factor which contributed to Miskito political attitudes was that for them, the original experience with the Sandinistas along the Rio Coco had been negative. They personally knew American plantation managers and other foreigners, whom they generally admired, who were killed by guerrillas. Sandinista attacks devastated the Standard Fruit Company installations in April 1931, which directly hurt the Miskito smallholders who sold bananas to the company. Far from feeling exploited by Standard Fruit, the Miskito were delighted to have a market for their products and a chance to buy consumer goods in the company commissary at Puerto Cabo Gracias a Dios. Drawn into the wage economy during the last 100 years, the Miskito strongly identified with the companies and with their foreign managers. Miskito men . . . spoke admiringly of their former bosses. They also compared what they regarded as the good wages and the fair treatment as equals they had received from them, with the poor wages and treatment as social inferiors they say they receive from current Spanish-speaking Nicaraguan employers. In general, the Miskito did not feel exploited or oppressed by the foreign companies and did not share the Sandinista interpretation of them as class enemies of the people. In fact, one of their main concerns today is to bring the companies back so they can have jobs and good wages again (Dennis, 1981:283–84).

The dramatic decline in the operations of American firms in Nicaragua during the 1930s was also a product of the worldwide depression of that decade and of other factors associated with resource depletion, but the prevailing interpretation on the Atlantic Coast was that it was the result of Sandino's attacks (Bourgois, 1981:31). The religious situation was another contributing factor to the tense ethnic relations.

The implacable opposition of the Amerindian population to Spanish colonial penetration manifested itself as well in their resistance to conversion to the Catholic religion. To the Miskitu, the Catholic religion symbolized Spanish imposition and was met with unequivocal rejection. It was not until the arrival in 1849 of the Moravian church, a protestant faith from Germany, that Christian proselytizing in the Mosquitia took root. By 1900, scarcely half a century later, the majority of the Miskitu and Sumu communities had abandoned their traditional religion in favor of the Moravians. Adherence to the protestant faith was an expression of opposition to "Spanish" domination. Significantly, today, in blatant contrast to the deeply rooted Catholicism of the Ladino [mestizo] population of Nicaragua, the majority of the Costeños have maintained a firm adherence to the Moravian church. Even though perhaps 25 percent of the Miskitu have since entered the Catholic church—significantly through contact with North American and not Ladino missionaries—there is a profound equivalence between "being Miskitu" and the Moravian brotherhood. The Moravian faith, therefore, has developed into what could be called a national religion. Unfortunately the Moravian church is by no means unequivocally progressive. Certain of the less principlied Moravian leaders severely compromised themselves by cooperating with the Somoza regime. The sermons broadcast by the Moravian church from Honduras have been almost openly counterrevolutionary (ibid., 31; see also Jenkins Molieri, 1986:Chapter 2).

The stratification system that has developed on the Atlantic Coast, alluded to earlier, is another factor that must be taken into account, since it places Miskitu and other indigenous groups at the bottom of the social ladder. This is further complicated by the post–

World War II influx of mestizos to the coast, which has had the effect of putting pressure on lands traditionally claimed by the Miskitu. Finally, there is the question of the Miskitu people's relations with the Somoza regime and the revolutionary movement. Although the Atlantic Coast as a whole did not benefit from the policies of the Somoza government, Somoza himself apparently developed a patronage system with a number of Miskitu leaders. He also recruited Miskitu men for his National Guard, apparently on the assumption that their warrior tradition and their animosity toward mestizo Nicaraguans would make them an effective military force for maintaining himself in power (Dennis, 1981:282–83, 292). As a result of this and other factors mentioned above, the Atlantic Coast people in general did not participate actively in the Sandinista revolution. When the revolution succeeded, they were not integrated into the FSLN and did not identify with the revolution's goals.

All of these conditions, then, set the stage for the events that took place after 1979, and loaded the dice against smooth transition under the difficult conditions facing the new government.

The Sandinista Experience

The FSLN, far from being the monolithic totalitarian entity conjured up in the more florid phrases of the Reagan administration, is a broad popular coalition with a number of important ideological sources, among which are nationalism, democratic socialism, and liberation theology. The goals and policies it has articulated include nonalignment and self-determination, by which is meant basically freedom from domination by any external power, particularly the ever-present United States. This policy has had to be somewhat modified by the contra war, which forced the government to rely on military and logistical support from the Soviet bloc, but it has also attempted to maintain a broad base of international support from any country willing to help out. Other priorities include economic development, the maintenance of a mixed economy, and the provision of essential social services to the general populace. The FSLN has explicitly rejected the model of a one-party state, and has expressed commitment to the development of a pluralistic democratic system, difficult as that may be, given Nicaragua's political history (see Republic of Nicaragua, *Philosophy and Policies of the Government of Nicaragua*, 1982).

For the Atlantic Coast, the Sandinistas wished to overcome its historic separation from the rest of the country, to bring it into the revolutionary process, and to spur its economic development. This was perceived as beneficial to the Costeños and to the country as a whole. As we have seen, these plans soon ran afoul of historically conditioned barriers, mutual misunderstanding, some serious initial errors, and the contra war. Still, the overall record of the government clearly indicates flexibility and a willingness to respond to the demands of the residents of the Atlantic Coast. Demands for educational programs in the minority languages have been granted (Bourgois, 1981:26). A number of economic and social-development programs have been launched, limited as they may be by wartime scarcities. These programs include health care, the building of transportation networks, electricity, and the stimulation of coast industries such as fishing. Important measures have been taken to protect the damaged ecology of the region (Dunbar Ortiz, 1984:217, 240). In addition, Nicaragua has ratified all United Nations covenants and other instruments of international law dealing with human rights and the rights of indigenous communities, something the United States has not done (ibid., 228; Diaz-Polanco and Lopez y Rivas, 1986:172).

Some of the greatest obstacles in the postrevolutionary era were subjective ones. On the Sandinista side was a profound lack of knowledge about the minority communities of the Atlantic Coast, given the historical isolation of that region from the Pacific Coast. This ignorance, and a lack of facility in the minority languages, made communication and mutual understanding exceedingly difficult. In addition, the FSLN activists perceived the world through an ideological framework in which class relations were given a great deal of emphasis, and ethnic relations very little. In this view, the Costeños represented the oppressed classes of workers and peasants, a status they shared with the bulk of the mestizos on the Pacific Coast. Sandinista ideology was also focused on Nicaragua's economic underdevelopment and the ways in which that had been shaped by exploitative relations with countries such as Britain and the United States.

Given this framework, it was assumed that the minority communities would identify with other oppressed sectors of the Nicaraguan population, join existing Sandinista popular, mass-based organizations, and participate in the continuing revolutionary struggle against imperialism and class oppression. It was also assumed that economic development would solve the problem of interethnic relations (Gordon, 1985:133–36; Gurdian and Hale, 1985:144; Martinez, 1986:4).

Indigenous groups such as the Miskitus, on the other hand, did not see the social world primarily in class terms. Instead, ethnic relations were assigned a high priority, with Miskitus as a whole seen as a group historically oppressed by mestizos as a whole. In addition, there was little awareness of imperialism, and past relations with England and the United States were generally perceived as benign. What resulted, then, was a defense of traditional institutions and a multiclass solidarity around organizations such as MISURASATA, rather than a joining of Sandinista organizations (Gordon, 1985:135; Gurdian and Hale, 1985:144–45).

In addition, the Sandinistas were well aware that few Costeños had participated actively in the revolution, and that revolutionary ideology was not widespread on the coast. As a result, the government was reluctant to appoint Costeños to staff public-sector organizations in that region, instead bringing in politically trustworthy and well-qualified mestizos from the Pacific region. This practice in turn confirmed the perception of the minority groups that the mestizos were prejudiced against them (Gordon, 1985:133).

Given all of these factors, it is not surprising that conflict broke out on the Atlantic Coast, and that this area has still been only partially brought into the revolutionary process. Still, it is possible to see a considerable evolution of thinking on the part of the FSLN in the period from 1981 to 1986. The first significant statement on these issues emerged in 1981 as the *Declaration of Principles of the Popular Sandinista Revolution in Regards to the Indigenous Communities of the Atlantic Coast*. Among other things, it states:

All citizens of Nicaragua, regardless of race or religion, shall enjoy equal rights. The Revolution will actively fight and oppose all forms of racial, linguistic and cultural discrimination in the national territory. Wherever racism may sprout this government shall support the fight against it.

The Government of National Reconstruction, convinced of the need to rescue and nurture the different cultural manifestations, present in the national territory, will provide the Miskito, Creole, Sumu and Rama communities of the Atlantic coast with the means that are required to develop and enhance their cultural traditions, including the preservation of their languages.

The Popular Sandinista Revolution will not only guarantee but also legalize the ownership of lands on which the people of the communities of the Atlantic Coast have traditionally lived and worked, organized either as communities or cooperatives. Land titles will be granted to each community (Dunbar Ortiz, 1984:273–74).

Since 1984, the keystone to governmental policy toward the coast has been regional autonomy.

Toward Regional Autonomy

In a startling departure from the policies of previous governments, and in a move unprecedented in the Americas, a National Commission on Regional Autonomy was established in Nicaragua in 1984. Shortly thereafter, two regional autonomy commissions were formed, one for Special Zone I (Zelaya Norte, or the northern Atlantic Coast) and one for Special Zone II (Zelaya Sur, or the southern zone). This commission and its two subcommissions were charged with coming up with a solution to the problem of interethnic and regional relations that would promote integration and development in a nonassimilationist and noncoercive manner. In 1985, the national Autonomy Commission published a preliminary document entitled *Principles and Policies for the Exercise of the Right of Autonomy by the Indigenous People and Communities of the Atlantic Coast of Nicaragua*. This short document was widely disseminated and was the basis for extensive consultations with the minority communities of the Atlantic Coast.

The first concrete result of these activities was the recognition of the rights of minority peoples in Nicaragua's new Constitution, adopted in 1987. This Constitution explicitly recognizes the multiethnic and multilingual character of Nicaragua (*Constitution of the Republic of Nicaragua*, Articles 8 and 11). It outlaws discrimination on the basis of nationality, race, or language, and gives recognition to the Universal Declaration of Human Rights (Articles 27, 46, and 91). Article 89 states, in part:

The Communities of the Atlantic Coast have the right to preserve and develop their cultural identities within the framework of national unity, to be granted their own forms of social organization, and to administer their local affairs according to their traditions.

Article 90 adds:

The communities of the Atlantic Coast have the right to the free expression and preservation of their languages, art and culture. The development of their culture and values enriches the national culture. The state shall create special programs to enhance the exercise of these rights.

The statute on Atlantic Coast autonomy was adopted by the national legislature in October of 1987. This law established two autonomous regions for the Atlantic Coast area, one for the northern and one for the southern region. Citizens of the autonomous regions participate equally in all the rights and privileges granted to citizens in other parts of Nicaragua but also benefit from special rights corresponding to their distinctive ethnic identities.

The autonomy law grants official status to the minority languages within the autonomous regions, and gives minorities the right to be educated in their own languages. It establishes regional governments for the two areas, each to be headed by an elected legislative body called a Regional Council, and an executive body, the Regional Coordinator. The regional governments have taxing authority and are charged with passing regional laws and implementing national laws within their territories. Within the general framework of the national Constitution and laws, the regional governments are given broad responsibilities in the areas of economic, social, cultural, and defense policies. They are to oversee, in consultation with the national government, the use and development of the natural resources of the area, and to encourage the full participation of women in political, economic, and cultural life.

In addition, the law recognizes the legitimacy of traditional communal property holdings in the Atlantic Coast communities, and establishes a Special Development Fund for the benefit of the autonomous regions (Law of Autonomy of the Atlantic Coast Regions of Nicaragua).

Conclusion

Although the regional autonomy process is quite new in Nicaragua, the problems that it addresses are quite old. Thus, it will be some time before it will be possible to assess the success of this social experiment. Still, the Nicaraguans have demonstrated not only a strong will to resolve the problems of interethnic relations that have plagued the country for so long but also have shown considerable ingenuity and creativity in their approach. They have been bound neither by traditional Nicaraguan attitudes to the problem nor by the sometimes mechanical approaches and solutions that can be found in the socialist tradition. The Sandinista approach has been a flexible one, drawing on the experiences of other countries but adapting the solution to their particular circumstances and avoiding dogma and rhetoric. It is an experiment that should be watched and studied intently by minorities in other countries, for a successful regional autonomy program in Nicaragua would be a tremendous advance for the right of self-determination of minority peoples everywhere.

9

In Search of Aztlan

In the last two chapters, I have reviewed the situations of four countries that have experimented with what might be called a *pluralistic accommodation* among their ethnic and racial groups. Ideally, in such an arrangement the various groups can each strive for an equitable share of the country's resources without feeling that they must sacrifice their distinctive collective identities in the process. In other words, equality and community are not presented as an either-or choice, as has been the case in the United States and many other countries.

The advantages of this type of accommodation for the minority are apparent. As I argued in Chapters 2 through 5, Chicano ethnic goals have historically revolved around both equality and community, although different organizations have assigned the two goals different priorities. With an appropriate institutional arrangement, it would be at least theoretically possible to achieve both goals simultaneously. In the absence of such an accommodation, Chicanos have increasingly adopted strategies of individual upward mobility that result in assimilation and the dilution of the group's collective identity. The effects of this unfortunate "Hobson's choice" were outlined in Chapter 6.

An argument can also be made for a pluralistic accommodation from the perspective of the majority, however. Cultural diversity, I would argue, is a worthwhile end in itself, enriching the lives of all members of the society by expanding the scope and range of social life in innumerable dimensions, including music, art, literature, food, styles of dress, philosophical outlooks, and general lifestyle. Such diversity makes a society more cosmopolitan and more interesting. Learning to appreciate the value of cultural diversity also makes a society more tolerant and more open, and can serve as an antidote to narrow nationalism and ethnocentrism.

Counterbalanced against such a view is the traditional fear of mainstream Americans that cultural diversity threatens the stability of the society. This fear can be seen as far back as the writings of Thomas Jefferson, who felt that a homogeneous population was necessary for building a successful republic in the New World (Takaki, 1979:39, 63). The sociologist Milton Gordon has traced out the long history of activism around "Anglo conformity" in American history, characterizing it as the dominant attitude toward non-English ethnic groups in this country (Gordon, 1964:Chapter 4). In its current form, this stance can be seen in the "English only" movement in the United States, led ironically enough by Japanese-American ex-senator S. I. Hayakawa. It is difficult to imagine a Swiss organization pushing "German only" and claiming that the existence of French and Italian speakers were threatening the integrity of that republic.

There is actually a tradition of thought in the United States that supports the concept of a pluralistic accommodation, although it is not as popular as the more assimilation-oriented traditions. This is the cultural pluralism position, originally expounded in 1915 by the Jewish philosopher Horace Kallen (Kallen, 1924). In a two-article series published in *The Nation* as "Democracy Versus the Melting-Pot," Kallen critiqued prevailing notions of assimilation and the Americanization programs then very much in vogue. He argued for cultural tolerance as an extension of American democratic and egalitarian ideals and painted the following picture of the model U.S. society:

Its form would be that of the federal republic; its substance a democracy of nationalities, cooperating voluntarily and autonomously through common institutions in the enterprise of self-realization through the perfection of men according to their kind. The common language of the commonwealth, the language of its great tradition, would be English, but each nationality would have for its emotional and involuntary life its own peculiar dialect or speech, its own individual and inevitable esthetic and intellectual forms (ibid., 124).

The coexistence of different cultures, he felt, was an important element contributing to creativity in American life. Other writers have followed in Kallen's footsteps, and the general idea of cultural or ethnic pluralism has some following in the liberal professions, although perhaps not much among the general public.

Although the values expressed in the cultural pluralism tradition are consistent with those I am advocating, it has remained a curiously incomplete intellectual concept, a kind of "cognition interruptus." As Milton Gordon has pointed out, the moral analysis carried out by Kallen and others is not grounded in a sociological analysis (Gordon, 1964:148). In particular, the concept of culture is virtually free-floating, with little appreciation of the relationship that exists between culture and social institutions. The idea seems to be that a multiplicity of cultures can be maintained in a society if there is a supportive set of attitudes toward doing so, that is, if people in the society simply agree that it would be good to have cultural pluralism. A more realistic analysis would take note of the fact that culture is rooted in and shaped by a whole range of institutions: the mass media, which transmit cultural attitudes in a very direct manner; the schools, with their impact on language learning; the corporations, which reward certain types of language skills and cultural attributes and penalize others; the government, which is a major employer itself and which sets policies affecting all of the other institutions. As the Quebecois well know, a "do-your-own-thing-on-your-own-time" attitude doesn't take you very far toward cultural pluralism if everyone knows that English is the only way to get ahead. To achieve a real rather than an illusory cultural pluralism, then, requires a set of supportive institutions, such as are found in Quebec and Switzerland but not in the United States (Abu-Laban and Mottershead, 1981).

Tracing out this line of argument thus leads us back to regional autonomy, which provides precisely that type of institutional framework—one that allows cultural diversity and self-determination without penalties. If one looks back at the Chicano movement, it is clear that a partial anticipation of this position existed, particularly in the call for community control and the development of alternative institutions. However, those concepts remained very localistic at that time, focusing on particular communities rather than regions. Even if successful, they would have provided too narrow a base for a true cultural pluralism.

The concept of "Aztlan" can also be seen as a partial anticipation of a regional autonomy position, but it remained vague and subject to varying interpretations. None of the programmatic statements of the 1960s and early 1970s spelled out a clear orientation to the question of territorial and institutional control. Indeed, the whole "cultural nationalist" orientation suffered from the same weakness that has historically afflicted the cultural pluralism position—a lack of appreciation of the dynamic interrelationship of culture and institutions. Both sets of concepts have remained essentially voluntaristic, conveying the attitude that "will" alone is enough to achieve the desired goal.

REGIONAL AUTONOMY AS AN ALTERNATIVE

Regional autonomy is clearly a kind of in-between solution to ethnic and nationalist demands, poised between separatism and secession on the one hand and assimilation without choice on the other. It is not very widely known in the United States that quite a number of countries have arrived at some sort of regional autonomy arrangement to accommodate their multiple nationalities. In a detailed legalistic article, Hannum and Lillich have surveyed a number of those cases and indicated the broad scope of arrangements that can be grouped under the general heading of regional autonomy. They examine in considerable detail the ways in which different governments have handled such variables as the allocation of executive, legislative, and judicial powers between central and regional governments and the specific governmental functions granted to each level. Matters of foreign affairs and defense, they note, are almost universally reserved to the central government. On the other hand, regional governments often exercise considerable descretion over police forces, land and natural resources, financial and economic arrangements, and culture and religion. They also note special cases such as that of Belgium, where "linguistic communities" have been established to exercise a certain amount of cultural control without having a wide range of other political powers (Hannum and Lillich, 1980). They conclude with the following statement:

Although arriving at a firm definition that is appropriate in all cases is impossible, it is helpful to identify the *minimum* governmental powers that a territory would need to possess if it were to be considered fully autonomous and self-governing. Based on the entities surveyed, it is suggested that the following principles would be applicable to a fully autonomous territory:

(1) There should exist a locally elected body with some independent legislative power, although the extent of the body's competence will be limited by a constituent document. Within the realm of its competence—which should include authority over local matters such as health, education, social services, local taxation, internal trade and commerce, environmental protection, zoning, and local government structure and organization—the local legislative body should be independent, and its decisions should not be subject to veto by the principal/sovereign government unless those decisions exceed its competence or are otherwise inconsistent with basic constitutional precepts.

(2) There should be a locally chosen chief executive, possibly subject to approval or confirmation by the principal government, who has general responsibility for the administration and execution of local laws or decrees. The local executive may be given the authority to implement appropriate national/federal laws and regulations, although this is not a necessary power to attain autonomy.

(3) There should be an independent local judiciary, some members of which may also be subject to approval or confirmation by the central/principal government, with jurisdiction over purely local matters. Questions involving the scope of local power or the relationship between the autonomous and principal governments may be considered by either local or national courts in the first instance and generally may be appealed to a nonlocal court or a joint commission of some kind for final resolution.

(4) The status of autonomy and at least partial self-government is not inconsistent with the denial of any local authority over specific areas of special concern to the principal/sovereign government, as opposed to the reservation by the sovereign discretionary powers. Among the cases surveyed, for example, specific provision has been made for central governmental participation in or control over matters such as foreign relations; national defense; customs; immigration; security of borders and frontiers; airports and ports; interprovincial water and energy resources; general norms of civil, criminal, corporate, and financial behavior, as expressed in national legislation; restrictions on the taxing or debt-issuing authority of the autonomous entity; monetary, banking, and general economic policy; and interprovincial or extraprovincial commerce. In addition, the central government has the power of eminent domain for public works and must approve any proposed amendment to the constitution or other basic constituent document.

(5) Full autonomy and self-government also are consistent with power-sharing arrangements between the central and autonomous governments in such areas as control over ports and other aspects of transportation, police powers, exploitation of natural resources, and implementation of national/central legislation and regulations (Hannum and Lillich, 1980:886-87).

In the present work, we have examined four examples of such arrangements, representing several degrees of autonomy. Two of these fall into the category of what might be termed *implicit regional autonomy.* In both Canada and Switzerland, a federal system of government has combined with the coexistence of different ethnic groups to produce a system of ethnic regional autonomy that is not called by that name. In the case of Canada, it came about as a compromise resolution to the demands for greater self-determination on the part of the francophone minority, a sector of whom had called for more radical solutions such as sovereignty or "sovereignty-association." Regional autonomy here was a grudging concession that emerged out of struggle and continues to be a source of conflict.

In the case of Switzerland, the system is more highly developed and has been in existence for a longer period of time, evolving over several centuries as a gradual fusing of previously independent states and peoples. If nothing else, the Swiss example shows that it is possible to work out a system of regional autonomy that operates equitably and democratically, at least under Swiss conditions. Other countries in addition to Canada and Switzerland have a form of implicit regional autonomy, such as Yugoslavia, but it has not been possible to examine that experience in the present work.

Under the category *explicit regional autonomy,* we have looked at the established system of China and the emerging system of Nicaragua. As we saw, the Chinese case has many positive features but suffers from the drawback that the guiding, although only semi-articulated, ideology still foresees a gradual assimilation process taking place in that country. Here short-run cultural pluralism and regional autonomy become long-run "Han-conformity" via "natural" sociological processes. The Nicaraguan example provides us with the first explicit regional-autonomy framework in the Western Hemisphere—and may well serve as a model for other countries— but the situation there is too new and too fluid to tell us very much as yet. Again, other countries with explicit systems of regional autonomy exist, but it was not possible to look at them within the scope of this study. Spain, for example, has such a system, with antecedents dating back to the 1930s, when Catalonia was granted limited regional autonomy. The present system there dates from the 1970s and includes the Basque and other regions. The question remains as to the relevance of this whole discussion for the United States.

At this point, it would be well to point out that the system of regional autonomy is not intended to solve all social problems confronting a particular group. Other political questions, such as those involving class-based and gender-based inequalities, are left unresolved by this arrangement. Regional autonomy focuses specifically on the question of attaining an equitable and pluralistic accommodation among cultural and racial groups in a multiethnic society. Nevertheless, my own feeling is that any movement that aims at greater equality is a good thing. Once a specific condition of inequality begins to be questioned, it becomes easier to extend the argument to other social realms and to elevate equality to a general principle.

THE QUESTION OF APPLICABILITY

Some general arguments can be anticipated concerning the feasibility of regional autonomy in the context of the United States. In the first instance, it can be argued that a certain cost is involved in establishing a new administrative system. To this, one can reply that if countries like China and Nicaragua can bear those costs, the United States should probably be able to do so as well. There are also practical difficulties involved with the fact that ethnic groups overlap in their patterns of residence, so that it is not possible to draw neat boundaries around regions. This is the type of argument that the Quebecois call mappism. Here again, one can point to the Chinese example, where the patterns of ethnic group settlement are extremely complex. In some areas, there are situations in which one ethnic group lives in the valleys and another on the ridges of hills, and so on. The Chinese have dealt with this complexity by allowing for regional autonomy areas of different sizes, and in some cases, even having a regional autonomy area for one group within the boundaries of a regional autonomy area for another group. If the will is present, these kinds of troublesome difficulties can be resolved.

It may also be argued that regional autonomy may work well in relatively less-developed countries, where groups are more settled and there is less mobility than in highly industrial systems. It was partly in anticipation of this point that I included such industrial societies as Canada and Switzerland in the discussion.

Perhaps more difficult to answer are questions about whether conditions exist in the United States that would allow regional autonomy to ever become a realistic political possibility for groups such as Chicanos. In order to respond to this, we need to consider a number of factors.

Clearly, one of the most important conditions has to do with patterns of settlement and degree of concentration of the ethnic minorities. In the four countries studied here, the most important minority groups occupy geographic areas in which they have historic ties—in some cases, for many centuries. Generally, they also form a local majority, although that is not true for some of the Chinese groups. Perhaps the comparison with Quebec is most apt. Francophones constitute some 80 percent of the population of Quebec, whereas Chicanos at the present time do not form a majority in any U.S. state. In this respect, Francophones were fortunate than non-French-speaking immigrants to Quebec often moved on to more western provinces in search of open land and other economic opportunities. Chicanos, on the other hand, have been concentrated in the western part of the United States, so the pattern in the last century has been for more and more non-Chicanos to move in from the rest of the country. That trend is now being counterbalanced by increased immigration from Mexico and other parts of Latin America, and by the higher fertility rates of U.S. Latinos as compared to the general population. So, although the proportion of Chicanos in the Southwest declined for the earlier period, it is now again on the rise.

The three areas that would seem to be the most likely candidates for Chicano regional-autonomy areas are southern California, northern New Mexico, and southern Texas. In the case of California, the 1980 U.S. Census indicated that 19.2 percent of the state's population fell into the category of Spanish/Hispanic Origin (Bris-

Table 9.1

California: Projected Population by Race/Ethnicity, 1980 to 2030 (percent)

	1980	1990	2000	2010	2020	2030
Non-Hispanic White	66.5	58.8	52.4	47.0	43.8	38.4
Black	7.5	7.5	7.4	7.2	7.2	6.7
Hispanic	19.2	24.2	28.5	32.2	33.3	38.1
Asians	5.6	8.3	10.6	12.5	14.6	15.6
Others	1.2	1.2	1.1	1.1	1.1	1.2
Total	100.0	100.0	100.0	100.0	100.0	100.0

Source: Adapted from Leon Bouvier and Philip Martin, *Population Change and California's Future* (Washington, D.C.: Population Reference Bureau, 1985), p. 13. Reprinted with permission.

chetto, 1984:141). However, various projections have pointed to a dramatic rise in that proportion in the next twenty to fifty years. A 1985 study predicts that the Hispanic population of California (most of which is Chicano) will rise to 28.5 percent of the state's total by 2000, and to 38.1 percent by 2030 (Bouvier and Martin, 1985); (see Table 9.1). A separate set of projections up to the year 2020, by the California Department of Finance, comes to very similar conclusions (Caiifornia Department of Finance, 1986).

The Spanish/Hispanic–origin population of California, which is largely Chicano, is not evenly distributed throughout the state. The Bouvier and Martin study cited above estimates that by the year 2000, the Los Angeles–Long Beach–Anaheim Standard Consolidated Area (a U.S. Census designation) will have a 34.5 percent Hispanic population. For the year 2030, they project a Hispanic population for that same area of 44.8 percent, by which time the white population would have shrunk to 33 percent (Bouvier and Martin, 1985:20).

A 1984 study by the Southern California Association of Governments (SCAG) points to the same general conclusions. That study is based on an area of southern California that includes the coun-

Table 9.2

Ethnic Population in the SCAG Region (counties of Los Angeles, Ventura, Orange, San Bernardino, Riverside, and Imperial)

	1980	2000			
		LOW	MOD-LOW	MOD-HI	HIGH
Non-Hispanic White % of Total	60.6	51.6	49.7	46.9	41.9
Hispanic % of Total	24.2	30.5	32.8	35.2	41.0
Black % of Total	9.0	9.2	8.9	8.5	7.7
Asian/Other % of Total	6.2	8.7	8.6	9.4	9.3

Source: Adapted from Southern California Association of Governments, "Ethnic Population in the SCAG Region," Southern California: A Region in Transition, Vol. 1 (1984), p. 14. Reprinted with permission.

ties of Los Angeles, Ventura, Orange, San Bernardino, Riverside, and Imperial. Their projections are reproduced below in Table 9.2, and are based on four different scenarios for the 1980–2000 period, with the variation being accounted for by different assumptions about immigration levels.

The current regional distribution of Chicanos in California can be seen by examining Figure 9.1, which shows levels of concentration at the county level.

The 1980 Census indicated that the proportion of Hispanics in the state of New Mexico was 36.6 percent (Brischetto, 1984:141). As can be seen from examining Figure 9.2, the distribution pattern is quite different from California, with eight out of the thirty-two counties already having a concentration of Hispanics over 50 percent, and another thirteen being in the 30–49 percent range. Given its long history of Chicano settlement and its distinctive regional flavor, northern New Mexico would appear to be a leading candidate for a future ethnic-autonomy area. New Mexico Chicanos also have more of a multiclass nature than is true in many other parts

Figure 9.1
California: Percent Spanish Origin by County, 1980

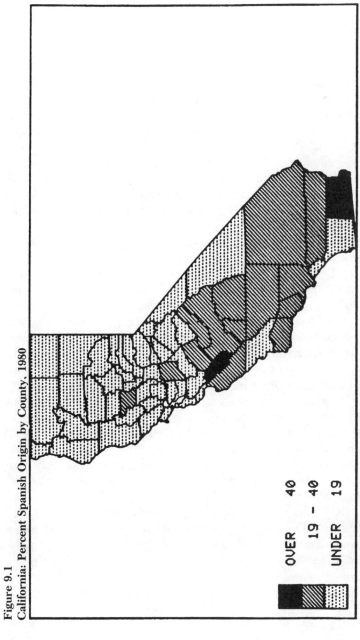

OVER 40

19 – 40

UNDER 19

Source: Census of Population and Housing, 1980: STF1A.

of the Southwest, and their level of political organization is indicated by the fact that a recent governor of New Mexico, Tony Anaya, is a Chicano.

The proportion of Hispanic/Spanish origin in Texas in 1980 is listed by the U.S. Census as 21 percent, which is close to that of California (ibid.). However, the pattern of regional distribution is quite different, with a very heavy concentration in the southern part of the state. In 1980, Texas had ten counties that were over 80 percent Chicano, with another eleven in the 60–79 percent range (see Figure 9.3). The Texas Department of Health estimates that by the year 2000, the Hispanic proportion of the state's population will have increased to 24 percent (Texas Department of Health, 1985).

Demographic trends, then, indicate that certain parts of the Southwest will become increasingly suitable for ethnic autonomy areas. Equally important in assessing prospects are variables having to do with the attitudes and ideologies on the part of both minorities and majorities. In the case of the most equitable accommodation, that of Switzerland, gradual developments over the course of several centuries have allowed all of the major constituent groups to work out an intricate system based on a good deal of flexibility and trust. In the case of Nicaragua, the leadership has no doubt been moved toward a regional autonomy tradition by their identification with socialist ideals and the fact that other socialist countries, such as China, have previously adopted such a system. In the United States, neither of these conditions prevails, and there is no doubt that a political movement for regional autonomy would encounter a great deal of resistance. Still, as the Quebecois have shown, a determined struggle can produce results in a relatively inhospitable environment.

Another major question at the subjective level has to do with whether Chicano attitudes would ever favor a move toward such a solution. For many Chicanos, the U.S. Southwest is seen as a historic homeland; and in some parts, such as northern New Mexico, there has been a continuous and significant presence for several centuries. On the other hand, as pointed out in Chapter 6, a great deal of integration and assimilation has already taken place, and this development is at least tacitly accepted by a certain proportion of the group. The Chicano situation is also complicated by the con-

Figure 9.2
New Mexico: Percent Spanish Origin by County, 1980

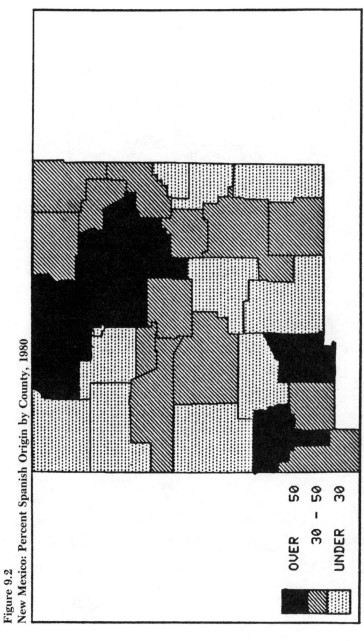

OVER 50

30 – 50

UNDER 30

Source: Census of Population and Housing, 1980: STF1A.

Figure 9.3
Texas: Percent Spanish Origin by County, 1980

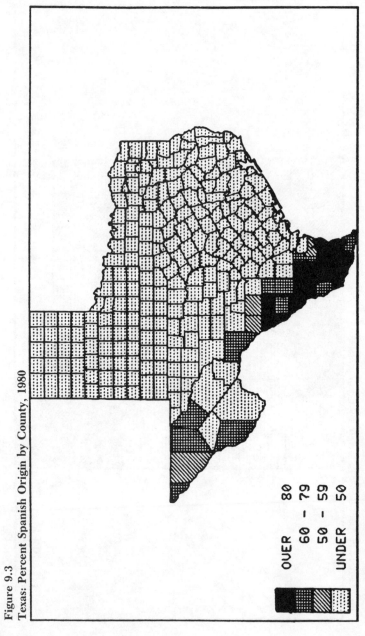

OVER 80
60 - 79
50 - 59
UNDER 50

Source: Census of Population and Housing, 1980: STF1A.

tinuing in-migration to the Southwest from Mexico and the resulting presence of several different generations with varying attitudes and cultural styles. Still, attitudes of this nature are notoriously difficult to predict—witness the fact that no one predicted the Chicano Movement before it happened, nor the Quiet Revolution in Quebec. A political ideology or movement that seems highly improbable under present conditions may come to life as conditions change, and demographic patterns are certainly changing.

In this connection, it is well to take note of the role played by intellectuals and other professionals in ethnic movements. Such movements often receive an important impetus from professional groups who see it as being in their interest to mobilize an ethnic constituency in order to achieve their goals. This was the case in Quebec, as pointed out in Chapter 7, when a rising strata of Quebecois professionals and administrators found their path blocked by the established order with its ethnic stratification system. The British sociologist Anthony Smith has shown how general a phenomenon this is in his recent survey of the "ethnic revival" (Smith, 1981:Chapter 6). Intellectuals play a key role in this type of movement, since it is they who are able to work and rework the symbols that are so important in creating or reinterpreting the collective sense of identity. In the Chicano Movement of the 1960s, key intellectuals such as the playwright Luis Valdez and the poet Alurista played major behind-the-scenes roles in such early political events as the Denver Youth Conference in 1969 (Alurista, interview, August, 1982). The significance of all this is that it has been only recently that a sizable number of Chicano professionals and intellectuals has emerged, and the role they will play in setting the future political direction of the group has yet to be determined. Chicano intellectuals as an organized group have existed only since the early 1970s. Prior to that time, there were only scattered Chicano intellectuals, working in virtual isolation, whereas now there are Chicano journals, Chicanos Studies programs, and a National Association for Chicano Studies, as well as a host of professional organizations of various types. At a certain point, given favorable conditions, these strata may play a leading role in reformulating Chicano ethnic goals.

If ethnic autonomy does become part of the Chicano political agenda at some future point, there are two general routes it could take. One is the explicit model, which would require the designation of special areas specifically for ethnic autonomy, and would be a modification of the existing federal system. The other route would be to work for the redrawing of state lines, carving out new states that would have a majority or plurality Chicano population. This route would be more along the Canadian or Swiss model, in that it would not necessarily require a change in existing federal principles. The case of the Swiss Jura, discussed in Chapter 8, provides a very close parallel. In passing, it might be noted that the idea of dividing California into more than one state is not a new idea. In the years prior to 1915, many such efforts originated in southern California. Since then, a number of others have come from the northern part of the state (Hillinger, 1986).

THE SHORT, THE MEDIUM, AND THE LONG RUN

Although the general thrust of my argument has been to favor a regional autonomy solution to U.S. ethnic and racial problems, it is clear that the present climate of opinion makes such a solution impossible in the short run. It would be more helpful at this time to think in terms of a sequential strategy that would lead in that direction by a series of smaller steps.

The Short Run

Conditions during the 1980s have been quite unfavorable for the advancement of Chicano interests. The degree of activism has been low, and it is not at all clear whether the slow process of occupational upgrading that characterized the 1940–1970 period has continued. The conservative atmosphere associated with the Reagan administrations has made it difficult to sustain any kind of progressive movements. In addition, high and persistent rates of unemployment have led to a considerble degree of frustration among Anglo workers, and that has made it easy for opportunistic politicians to use Latinos and other minorities as scapegoats. One direction this has taken has been an emotional campaign for immigration restrictions. Another has been the "English only" movement,

Figure 9.4
Published Advertisement for Proposition 63 in California

ONE NATION, ONE LANGUAGE

Generations of immigrants to the United States have learned English in order to take their places as citizens of their adopted land. But today our country is in danger of being split apart by language divisions.

That is why English First urges you to vote for Proposition 63, to make English the official state language of California.

A Nation Divided

The leaders of the bilingual movement reject the concept of the "melting pot." Against the wishes of the vast majority of Americans, they demand we officially become a multilingual, multicultural nation. They have already succeeded in forcing on us bilingual education, multilingual ballots, and widespread use of other languages in public situations—all at great expense to the taxpayer.

To see where this leads, we have only to look at Canada, which has been officially bilingual since 1969. In Quebec, it is a *criminal offense* for companies not to give French equal billing with English. All official government statements must be translated into two languages and the political parties fight over which version is the correct one.

Canada is literally split apart by language. America will soon be equally divided if we do not act now.

Time To Take A Stand

It's time to declare English our official language. The passage of Proposition 63 will mean that the state government must func-

tion only in English, and protect English as the common language of the state.

Five other states have declared English the official language: Illinois, Indiana, Nebraska, Virginia and Kentucky. If California joins them by passing the Official Language Amendment, we will send a powerful message to Congress to take action on a national level—to repeal bilingual ballots and federally mandated bilingual education.

Don't let opponents of the Amendment scare you with misinformation. The Amendment *won't* affect what language is used in private situations—at home, at church, with your friends and in your business. It *won't* affect foreign language instruction.

And it is *not* racist or anti-foreign-born. By learning English, all immigrants will have a better opportunity to enter the mainstream of our society and to advance as far as their talents and capabilities can take them.

What Is English First?

English First is a national organization dedicated to making English the official language of the United States. We believe that California's decision to make English the official state language can powerfully influence Congress and the American people.

If you would like to find out more about us, or make a contribution to help pay for this statewide advertising campaign, please fill out the coupon below and send it to English First, 7672 Del Oak Way, Suite A, Sacramento, California 95831.

Source: San Francisco Chronicle, October 5, 1986.

which has succeeded in getting several midwestern and southern border states to declare English as their official language.

An examination of one of the ads for Proposition 63, which declared English to be the official language of California, is reproduced in Figure 9.4. The antibilingual ballot and antibilingual-education intent of this measure is made explicit in that ad. Interestingly enough, specific reference is made to Quebec, although the depiction of English and French as having coequal status there is factually incorrect.

In my opinion, the "English only" movement is a continuation of the long American tradition of ethnocentrism, Anglo-conformity, and cultural intolerance, and opposition to it should be a very high priority for all Latinos, Asians, other language minorities, and progressive groups in general.

The Medium Run

An appropriate medium-run goal for Latinos and other language minorities would be that of seeking official, legal recognition for the United States as a multicultural, multilingual country, the exact opposite of what "English only" proponents want. This is something that already exists in many countries, including the ones examined in the present work. One of the more important points that I hope has been conveyed in this book is that the existence of more than one culture in a country is not a source of division. Division comes from the perception of one group that it is not being treated fairly by another. Economic, political, and cultural oppression, and not multiculturalism, are the true sources of divisiveness.

A pro-multicultural movement could begin by aiming for such recognition at the statewide level, with the eventual goal of having such a provision adopted as an amendment to the U.S. Constitution.

Some precedents for this already exist: some state constitutions formally acknowledge the existence of more than one cultural group. The New Mexico Constitution, for example, requires that proposed constitutional amendments be published in both English- and Spanish-language newspapers. Article XII, Section 8 of the same document states:

The legislature shall provide for the training of teachers in the normal schools or otherwise so that they may become proficient in both the English and Spanish languages (*Constitutions of the United States*, 1982:82).

Article XX, Section 12 adds:

For the first twenty years after this Constitution goes into effect all laws passed by the legislature shall be published in both the English and Spanish languages and thereafter such publications shall be made as the legislature may provide (ibid, 86).

The Hawaii Constitution provides in its Article IX, Section 9 that "the State shall have the power to preserve and develop the cultural, creative and traditional arts of its various ethnic groups" (ibid., 1984:33) Article XV, Section 4 states:

English and Hawaiian shall be the official languages of Hawaii, except that Hawaiian shall be required for public acts and transactions only as provided by law (ibid., 1984:42).

The Long Run

Although it would be a positive step to have official recognition of multiculturalism in the United States, that in itself would not be enough to stabilize the status of minority languages and cultures. As I have argued above, such a stabilization would require a grounding in the social institutions of the country. Gaining legal status for multiculturalism would help prepare the ideological climate for an eventual campaign for ethnic regional autonomy, but that is something that would undoubtedly require a great deal of time and effort. Raising it as an issue prematurely would be counterproductive. Given enough time, however, it may be possible to educate people to the fact that such ethnic autonomy is not threatening to the territorial integrity of the United States, and that already it exists and functions well in a number of countries.

CONCLUSION

Ultimately, this has been a book about choices. I have sought to show that the prevailing social structure and ideology of the United States provide Chicanos and other ethnic minorities with only two very restricted choices: assimilate or suffer the consequences. The present path is toward assimilation, slow and indirect as it may be. For other choices to be possible, it will be necessary to change the structure and the ideology of the country, along lines that have already been explored in a number of other countries.

Both of the two major routes that have been outlined in the previous discussion involve a system of regional autonomy. The implicit form, as found in Canada and Switzerland, comes about when ethnic groups make use of a federal form of government to gain political control of regions and then use that control to establish policies favorable to their economic and cultural status. In the explicit form, seen in China and emerging in Nicaragua, regions where the ethnic groups are concentrated are formally designated as regional autonomous areas, with special provisions for minority control. Whether Chicanos in the United States will choose one or the other of these routes in the future is difficult to predict. I have not attempted to make such a prediction here, but I have tried to make clear that in the absence of such a development, it will be impossible to attain the ethnic goals that Chicano political organizations have historically articulated.

Bibliography

Abney-Guardado, Armando. "Chicano Intermarriage in the United States: A Sociocultural Analysis." Ph.D. dissertation, University of Notre Dame, 1983.

Abu-Laban, Baha, and Donald Mottershead. "Cultural Pluralism and Varieties of Ethnic Politics." *Canadian Ethnic Studies*, Vol. 13, No. 3 (1981):44–63.

Achor, Shirley. *Mexican Americans in a Dallas Barrio*. Tuscon: University of Arizona Press, 1978.

Acuña, Rodolfo. *Occupied America*. 2nd ed. New York: Harper & Row, 1981.

Adams, Richard. "The Sandinistas and the Indians."*Caribbean Review*, Vol. 10, No. 1 (1981):23–25, 55–56.

Aguirre, Adalberto, Jr. "Language Use Patterns of Adolescent Chicanos in a California Border Town," in F. Barkin, E. A. Brandt, and J. Ornstein-Galicia, eds., *Bilingualism and Language Contact: Spanish, English, and Native American Languages*. New York: Teachers College Press, 1982:278–89.

Alinsky, Saul. *Reveille for Radicals*. New York: Vintage books, 1969 (originally published in 1946).

———. *Rules for Radicals: A Practical Primer for Realistic Radicals*. New York: Vintage Books, 1972.

Allsup, Carl. "Education Is Our Freedom: The American G.I. Forum and the Mexican American School Segregation in Texas, 1948–1957." *Aztlan*, Vol. 8 (1977):29–49.

————. *The American G.I. Forum: Origins and Evolution.* Monograph No. 6. Austin: Center for Mexican American Studies, University of Texas, 1982.

Amastae, Jon. "Language Shift and Maintenance in the Lower Rio Grande Valley of Southern Texas," in F. Barkin, E. A. Brandt, and J. Ornstein-Galicia, eds., *Bilingualism and Language Contact: Spanish, English, and Native American Languages.* New York: Teachers College Press, 1982: 261–77.

Arce, Carlos, and Armando Abney. "Regional Differences in Chicago Intermarriage." *La Red/The Net,* No. 52 (March, 1982):2–3.

Arnopoulos, Sheila McLeod, and Dominique Clift. *The English Fact in Quebec.* 2d ed. Montreal: McGill Queen's University Press, 1984.

August Twenty-Ninth Movement. *Unity Statement.* Privately published, 1974.

————. *Fan the Flames.* Privtely published, ca. 1976.

Autonomy Commission. *Principles and Policies for the Exercise of the Right to Autonomy by the Indigenous People and Communities of the Atlantic Coast of Nicaragua.* July, 1985.

Avineri, Shlomo. *Karl Marx on Colonialism and Modernization.* Garden City, N.Y.: Anchor Books, 1969.

Banton, Michael. *Racial and Ethnic Competition.* Cambridge: Cambridge University Press, 1983.

Barber, Benjamin. *The Death of Communal Liberty: A History of Freedom in a Swiss Mountain Canton.* Princeton, N.J.: Princeton University, 1974.

Barrera, Mario. *Race and Class in the Southwest.* Notre Dame, Ind.: University of Notre Dame Press, 1979.

Bean, Frank, and Benjamin Bradshaw. "Intermarriage between Persons of Spanish and Non-Spanish Surname: Changes from the Mid-Nineteenth to the Mid-Twentieth Century." *Social Science Quarterly,* Vol. 51 (September, 1970):389–95.

Biberman, Jaime. "The Development of Capitalism in Nicaragua: A Political Economic History." *Latin American Perspectives,* Vol. 10, No. 1 (Winter, 1983):7–32.

Birnbaum, Norman. "Communist China's Policy toward Her Minority Nationalities, 1950–1965." Ph.D. dissertation, St. John's University, 1970.

Black, George. *Triumph of the People: The Sandinista Revolution in Nicaragua.* London: Zed Press, 1981.

Blaustein, Albert, ed. *Fundamental Legal Documents of Communist China.* South Hackensack, N.J.: Rothman, 1962.

Blawis, Patricia Bell. *Tijerina and the Land Grants.* New York: International Publishers, 1971.

Bourgois, Phillippe. "Class, Ethnicity, and the State among the Miskitu Amerindians of Northeastern Nicaragua." *Latin American Perspectives*, Vol. 8, No. 2 (Spring, 1981):22–39.

Bouvier, Leon, and Philip Martin. *Population Change and California's Future*. Washington, D.C.: Population Reference Bureau, 1985.

Brazeau, Jacques, and Edouard Cloutier. "Interethnic Relations and the Language Issue in Contemporary Canada: A General Appraisal," in Milton Esman, ed., *Ethnic Conflict in the Western World*. Ithaca, N.Y.: Cornell University Press, 1977:204–27.

Breton, Raymond, Jeffrey Reitz, and Victor Valentine. *Cultural Boundaries and the Cohesion of Canada*. Montreal: The Institute for Research on Public Policy, 1980.

Briegel, Kay. "Alianza Hispano-Americana, 1894–1965: A Mexican American Fraternal Insurance Society." Ph.D. dissertation, University of Southern California, 1974.

Briggs, Vernon, Walter Fogel, and Fred Schmidt. *The Chicano Worker*. Austin: The University of Texas, 1977.

Brischetto, Robert. "The Hispanic Electorates." in *The Hispanic Almanac*. New York: Hispanic Policy Development Project, 1984:139–52.

Burma, John H., Gary A. Cretser, and Ted Seacret. "A Comparison of the Occupational Status of Intramarrying and Intermarrying Couples: A Research Note." *Sociology and Social Research*, Vol. 54, No. 4 (July, 1970):508–19.

Burnstein, John. "Ethnic Minorities and the Sandinist Government." *Journal of International Affairs*, Vol. 36, No. 1 (Spring/Summer, 1982:155–62.

Burt, Kenneth. *The History of MAPA and Chicano Politics in California*. Sacramento, Calif.: Mexican American Political Association, 1982a.

———. "The History of the Mexican-American Political Association and Chicano Politics in California." Senior honors thesis, University of California, Berkeley, 1982b.

Butler, Judy. "Autonomia Para La Costa." *WANI*, No. 2–3 (December-May, 1985a):6–13.

———. "La Costa Voto: Los Costenos y las Elecciones." *WANI*, No. 2–3 (December-May, 1985b):27–31.

———. "Proyectos Pilotos de Autonomia Zonal."*WANI*, No. 4 (July–September, 1986):23–27.

California Department of Finance. *Projected Total Population for California by Race/Ethnicity, July 1, 1980 to July 1, 2020*. Report 86 P–4. Sacramento, CA: Population Research Unit, February, 1986.

Camarillo, Alberto. *Chicanos in a Changing Society: From Mexican Pueblos to American Barrios in Santa Barbara and Southern California, 1848–1930*. Cambridge: Harvard University Press, 1979.

Carty, Kenneth, and Peter Ward, eds. *Entering the Eighties: Canada in Crisis.* Toronto: Oxford University Press, 1980.

Castillo, Pedro, and Alberto Camarillo, eds. *Furia y Muerte: Los Bandidos Chicanos.* Monograph No. 4. Los Angeles: Aztlan Publications, Chicano Studies Center, University of California, 1973.

Cazares, Ralph, Edward Murguia, and W. Parker Frisbie. "Mexican American Intermarriage in a Nonmetropolitan Context." *Social Science Quarterly,* Vol. 65, No. 2 (June, 1984):626–34.

Chandler, Charles. "The Mexican-American Protest Movement in Texas." Ph.D. dissertation, Tulane University, 1968.

Chang, Edward. "Korean Minority in China: A Historical Overview of China's Minority Policy and Korean emigration." Unpublished paper, 1985.

Chang Chih-i. *A Discussion of the National Question in the Chinese Revolution and of Actual Nationalities Policy* (Draft 1956). Translated by George Moseley and comprising pp. 29–159 of *The Party and the National Question in China,* cited below (see Moseley, 1966a).

The Changing Profile of Mexican America. Claremont, CA: The Tomas Rivera Center, October, 1985.

Chavez, John. *The Lost Land: The Chicano Image of the Southwest.* Albuquerque: University of New Mexico, 1984.

Chicano Coordinating Council on Higher Education. *El Plan de Santa Barbara.* Oakland, Calif.: La Causa Publications, 1969.

China's Minority Nationalities (1). Beijing: China Reconstructs, 1984.

Chin Chen-wu. "Education of the Nationalities in Lungsheng Autonomous Hsien." United States Department of Commerce, Joint Publications Research Service. *JPRS Reports,* No. 15540 (October 2, 1962).

"Chinese Minority Peoples Have More Industrial Workers." *Survey of China Mainland Press.* No. 5373–5377 (May 14–18, 1973).

CIDCA (Centro de Investigaciones y Documentacion de la Costa Atlantica). *Demografia Costena: Notas Sobre la Historia Demografica y Poblacion Actual de los Grupos Etnicos de la Costa Atlantica Nicaraguense.* 1982.

Clift, Dominique. *Quebec Nationalism in Crisis.* Kingston: McGill Queen's University Press, 1982.

Congreso para Pueblos Unidos. *La Vision,* Vol. 1 (January, 1980).

Connor, Walker. *The National Question in Marxist-Leninist Theory and Strategy.* Princeton, N.J.: Princeton University Press, 1984.

Constitution of the Republic of Nicaragua, 1987.

Constitutions of the United States, National and State. Volume 4. Dobbs Ferry, N.Y.: Oceana Publications, 1982.

Constitutions of the United States, National and State, Volume 2. Dobbs Ferry, N.Y.: Oceana Publications, 1984.

Cortes, Carlos. "A History of Chicano Resistance and Revolution." Unpublished paper, April 23, 1971.

Cretser, Gary, and Joseph Leon, eds. *Intermarriage in the United States.* New York: The Haworth Press, 1982.

Crow, John E. *Mexican Americans in Comtemporary Arizona: A Social and Demographic View.* San Francisco: R and E Research Associates, 1975.

Cuellar, Alfredo. "A Social and Political History of the Mexican-American Population of Texas, 1929–1963." M.A. thesis, North Texas State University, Denton, Texas, 1969.

Daalder, Hans. "On Building Consociational Nations: The Cases of the Netherlands and Switzerland," in Kenneth McRae, ed., *Consociational Democracy.* Toronto: McClelland and Stewart, 1974: 107–22.

Dagodag, W. "Public Policy and the Housing Patterns of Urban Mexican-Americans, In Selected Cities of the Central Valley." Ph.D. dissertation, University of Oregon, 1972.

Darroch, A. Gordon. "Another Look at Ethnicity, Stratification and Social Mobility in Canada." *Canadian Journal of Sociology,* Vol. 4, No. 1 (1979):1–25.

———. "Urban Ethnicity in Canada: Personal Assimilation and Political Communities." *Canadian Review of Sociology and Anthropology,* Vol. 18, No. 1 (1981):93–100.

Davidson, William. "Black Carib (Garifuna) Habitats in Central America," in Mary Helms and Franklin Loveland, eds., *Frontier Adaptations in Lower Central America.* Philadelphia: Institute for the Study of Human Issues, 1976:85–94.

Deal, David Michael. "National Minority Policy in Southwest China, 1911–1965." Ph.D. dissertation, University of Washington, 1971.

De Francis, John. "National and Minority Policies." *Annals of the American Academy of Political and Social Science* (September, 1951):146–55.

———. "Community Coalition Mobilizing East L.A." *Los Angeles Times,* December 26, 1977.

———. "Latino Activists from UNO Turn Backs on Ballot Box,"*Los Angeles Times,* July 27, 1980.

———. "2 Latino Activists Travel Separate Paths," *Los Angeles Times,* July 29, 1983.

Dennis, Philip. "The Costeños and the Revolution in Nicaragua." *Journal of Interamerican Studies and World Affairs,* Vol. 23, No. 3 (August, 1981):217–96.

Diao, Richard. "The National Minorities of China and Their Relations with the Chinese Communist Regime," in Peter Kunstadter, ed.,

Southeast Asian Tribes, Minorities, and Nations. Princeton, N.J., Princeton University Press, 1967:169–201.

Diaz-Polanco, Hector, and Gilberto Lopez y Rivas. *Nicaragua: Autonomia y Revolucion.* Mexicali, Mex.: Juan Pablos, Editor, 1986.

Dion, Leon. *Quebec: The Unfinished Revolution.* Montreal: McGill Queen's University Press, 1976.

Documents of the Chicano Struggle. New York: Pathfinder Press, 1971.

Documents of the First Session of the First National People's Congress of the CPR. Peking: Foreign Language Press, 1955.

Dofny, Jacques. "Ethnic Cleavages, Labor Aristocracy and Nationalism in Quebec," in Edward Tiryakian and Ronald Rogowski, eds., *New Nationalisms of the Developed West.* Boston: Allen & Unwin, 1985:353–73.

Dreyer, June. "Traditional Minorities Elites and the CPR Elite Engaged in Minority Nationalities Work," in Robert Scalapino, ed., *Elites in the People's Republic of China.* Seattle: University of Washington Press, 1972.

———. *China's Forty Millions.* Cambridge: Harvard University Press, 1976.

Driedger, Leo, ed. *The Canadian Ethnic Mosaic.* Toronto: McClelland and Stewart, 1978.

Dunbar Ortiz, Roxanne. "The Miskito People, Ethnicity, and the Atlantic Coast." *Nicaraguan Perspectives* (Winter, 1982):14–19.

———. *Indians of the Americas: Human Rights and Self-determination.* New York: Praeger, 1984.

Dunn, James. " 'Consociational Democracy' and Language Conflict: A Comparison of the Belgian and Swiss Experiences." *Comparative Political Studies,* Vol. 5, No. 1 (Spring, 1972):3–39.

Eberhard, Wolfram. *China's Minorities: Yesterday and Today.* Belmont, CA.: Wadsworth, 1982.

Esman, Milton, "The Politics of Official Bilingualism in Canada," in William Beer and James Jacob, eds., *Language Policy and National Unity.* Totowa, N.J.: Rowman & Allanheld, 1985:45–66.

Featherman, David, and Robert Hauser. *Opportunity and Change.* New York: Academic Press, 1978.

Fenwick, Rudy. "Communal Politics in Quebec: Ethnic Segmentation and Support for Political Independence among French Quebecois." Ph.D. dissertation, Duke University, 1978.

———. "Social Change and Ethnic Nationalism: An Historical Analysis of the Separatist Movement in Quebec." *Comparative Studies in Society and History,* Vol. 23, No. 2 (April, 1981):196–216.

Fincher, E. B. *Spanish-Americans As a Political Force in New Mexico 1912–1950.* Ph.D. dissertation, New York University, 1950. Reprinted by Arno Press, 1974.

Fishman, Joshua. "The Ethnic Revival in the United States: Implications for the Mexican-American Community," in Walker Commer, ed., *Mexican Americans in Comparative Perspective*. Washington, D.C.: The Urban Institute Press, 1985:309–54.

Fishman, Joshua, Vladimir Nahirny, John Hofman, and Robert Hayden, eds. *Language Loyalty in the United States*. The Hague: Mouton, 1966.

Floyd, Mary Beth. "Spanish-Language Maintenance in Colorado," in F. Barkin, E. A. Brandt, and J. Ornstein-Galicia, eds., *Bilingualism and Language Contact: Spanish, English, and Native American Languages*. New York: Teachers College Press, 1982:290–303.

———. "Syntactic Research in Southwest Varieties of Spanish," in F. Barkin, E. A. Brandt, and J. Ornstein-Galicia, eds., *Bilingualism and Language Contact: Spanish, English, and Native American Languages*. New York: Teachers College Press, 1982:139–53.

Floyd, Troy. *The Anglo-Spanish Struggle for Mosquitia*. Albuquerque: University of New Mexico, 1967.

Foley, Douglas, et. al. *From Peones to Politicos: Ethnic Relations in a South Texas Town, 1900–1977*. Monograph No. 3. Austin, Tex.: Center for Mexican American Studies, University of Texas, 1977.

Fraga, Luis Ricardo. "Organizational Maintenance and Organizational Success: The League of United Latin American Citizens." Paper presented at the Annual Meeting of the American Political Science Association, Washington, D.C., 1980.

Garcia, F. Chris, and Rodolfo de la Garza. *The Chicano Political Experience*. North Scituate, Ma.: Duxbury Press, 1977.

Garcia, Ignacio. "Mexican American Youth Organization: Precursors of Change in Texas." Mexican American Studies and Research Center Working Paper No. 8. Tucson: University of Arizona, January, 1987.

———. "San Antonio." *Nuestro* (August, 1980):22–24.

Garcia, Juan R. "Midwest Mexicanos in the 1920s: Issues, Questions, and Direction." *The Social Science Journal*, Vol. 19, No. 2 (April, 1982):89–99.

Garcia, Mario. "Americans All: The Mexican American Generation and the Politics of Wartime Los Angeles, 1941–45." *Social Science Quarterly*, Vol. 65, No. 5 (June, 1984a):278–89.

———. "Mexican American Labor and the Left: The Asociacion Nacional Mexico-Americana, 1949–1954," in John Garcia, Theresa Cordova, and Juan Garcia, eds., *The Chicano Struggle*. Binghamton, N.Y.: Bilingual Press, 1984b:65–86.

———. "La Frontera: The Border as Symbol and Reality in Mexican-American Thought." *Mexican Studies/Estudios Mexicanos*, Vol. 1, No. 2 (Summer, 1985):195–225.

Garcia, Richard. "The Chicano Movement and the Mexican American Community, 1972–1978: An Interpretive Essay." *Socialist Review* (July–October, 1978a):117–36.

———. "Class, Consciousness, and Ideology—The Mexican Community of San Antonio, Texas: 1930–1940." *Aztlan*, Vol. 9 (Spring, Summer, Fall, 1978b):23–69.

Gardner, Richard. *Grito! Reies Tijerina and the New Mexico Land Grant War of 1967.* New York: Harper & Row, 1970.

Garza, Edward. "LULAC: League of United Latin American Citizens." M.A. thesis, Southwest Texas State Teachers College, 1951.

"General Program of the People's Republic of China for the Implementation of Regional Autonomy for Nationalities." *Policy Towards Nationalities of the PRC.* Peking: Foreign Language Press, 1953:1–13.

Gerlach, Allen. "Conditions along the Border—1915, The Plan of San Diego." *New Mexico Historical Review* (July, 1968):195–212.

Girod, Roger. "Switzerland: Geography of the Swiss Party System,"in Kenneth McRae, ed., *Consociational Democracy.* Toronto: McClelland and Stewart, 1974:207–25.

Gittler, Joseph. "Cultural Pluralism in Contemporary American Society." *International Journal of Group Tensions*, Vol. 4, No. 3 (September, 1974):322–45.

Goldman, Shifra, and Tomas Ybarra-Frausto. *Arte Chicano: A Comprehensive Annotated Bibliography of Chicano Art, 1965–1981.* Berkeley: Chicano Studies Library Publications Unit, University of California, 1985.

Goldstein, Jay, and Rita Bienvenue, eds. *Ethnicity and Ethnic Relations in Canada.* Toronto: Butterworth & Co., 1980.

Gomez-Quiñones, Juan. "Plan de San Diego Reviewed." *Aztlan*, Vol. 1, No. 1 (Spring, 1970):124–32.

———. *Mexican Students Por La Raza: The Chicano Student Movement in Southern California 1967–1977.* Santa Barbara, CA: Editorial La Causa, 1978.

Gonzales, Rodolfo. *I am Joaquin.* Privately published, 1967.

Gonzalez, Nancie. *The Spanish-Americans of New Mexico.* Rev. ed. Albuquerque: University of New Mexico Press, 1969.

Gordon, Edmund. "Etnicidad, Conciencia y Revolucion: La Cuestion Miskito-Creole en Nicaragua." *Encuentro*, No. 24–25 (April–September, 1985):117–38.

Gordon, Milton. *Assimilation in American Life.* New York: Oxford University Press, 1964.

Goyder, John. "Ethnicity and Class Identity: The Case of French- and

English-Speaking Canadians." *Ethnic and Racial Studies*, Vol. 6, No. 1 (January, 1983):72–89.

Grebler, Leo, Joan Moore, and Ralph Guzman. *The Mexican-American People*. New York: The Free Press, 1970.

Grenier, Gilles. "Shifts to English As Usual Language by Americans of Spanish Mother Tongue." *Social Science Quarterly*, Vol. 65, No. 2 (June, 1984):537–50.

Gretler, Armin, and Pierre-Emeric Mandl. *Values, Trends and Alternatives in Swiss Society*. New York: Praeger, 1973.

Guindon, Hubert. "The Modernization of Quebec and the Legitimacy of the Canadian State." *Canadian Review of Sociology and Anthropology*, Vol. 15, No. 2, 1978:227–45.

Gurdian, Galio, and Charles Hale. "Integracion O Participacion? El Proyecto de Autonomia Costeña en la Revolucion Popular Sandinista." *Encuentro*, No. 24–25 (April–September, 1985):139–49.

Gutierrez, David. "CASA in the Chicano Movement: A Study of Organizational Politics and Ideology in the Chicano Community, 1968–1978." Unpublished paper, 1982.

Guzman, Ralph. "Politics and Policies of the Mexican-American Community," in Eugene P. Dvorin and Arthur I. Misner, eds., *California Politics and Policies*. Palo Alto, Calif.: Addison-Wesley, 1966:350–84.

Hager, William. "The Plan of San Diego: Unrest on the Texas Border in 1915." *Arizona and the West* (Winter, 1963):327–36.

Hale, Charles. "Class and Ethnicity in Revolutionary Nicaragua: The Case of the Miskitu." Unpublished paper, 1983.

Hall, Raymond, ed. *Ethnic Autonomy—Comparative Dynamics*. New York: Pergamon Press, 1979.

Hannum, Hurst, and Richard Lillich. "The Concept of Autonomy in International Law." *The American Journal of International Law*, Vol. 74, No. 4 (October, 1980):858–89.

Harris, Charles, and Louis Sadler. "The Plan of San Diego and the Mexican-United States War Crisis of 1916: A Reexamination." *Hispanic American Historical Review*, Vol. 58, No. 3 (August, 1978):381–408.

Heath, Shirley Brice. "Language Policies: Patterns of Retention and Maintenance," in Walker Conner, ed., *Mexican-Americans in Comparative Perspective*. Washington, D.C.: The Urban Institute Press, 1985:257–82.

Heaton, William. "Inner Mongolia: 'Local Nationalism' and the Cultural Revolution." Paper presented at the Association for Asian Studies, Annual Conference, March 30, 1971.

————. "Inner Mongolia: Aftermath of the Revolution." *Current Scene*, Vol. 9, No. 4 (April, 1971):6–16.

Helms, M. W. *Asang: Adaptations to Culture Contact in a Miskito Community*. Gainesville: University of Florida Press, 1971.

Henripin, Jacques. "Quebec and the Demographic Dilemma of French Canadian Society," in Dale Thomson, ed., *Quebec Society and Politics: Views from the Inside*. Toronto: McClelland and Stewart, 1973:155–66.

Hernandez, Jose. "The Political Development of Mutual Aid Societies in the Mexican American Community: Ideals and Principles." Ph.D. dissertation, University of California, Riverside, March, 1979.

————. *Mutual Aid for Survival: The Case of the Mexican American*. Malabar, FL.: Robert E. Krieger Publishing Co., 1983.

Hernandez-Chavez, Eduardo, Andrew Cohen, and Anthony Beltrand, eds. *El Lenguaje de los Chicanos: Regional and Social Characteristics of Language Used by Mexican Americans*. Arlington, Va.: Center for Applied Linguistics, 1975.

Herz, J. Spencer. "Let There Be Tigers." Unpublished book-length manuscript on Tijerina and the Alianza, 1970. Copy on file at the Chicano Studies Library, University of California, Berkeley.

————. Lecture on Tijerina and the Alianza, University of California, Riverside, April 1971.

Hillinger, Charles. "Two Californias? A Split Decision." *San Francisco Chronicle*, August 25, 1986:6.

History of CASA. Internal document of the Centro de Accion Social Autonomo, Stanford University Library, Green collection. Written ca. 1978.

Holmes, Jack. *Politics in New Mexico*. Albuquerque: University of New Mexico Press, 1967.

Horowitz, Donald. "Patterns of Ethnic Separatism." *Comparative Studies in Society and History*, Vol. 23, No. 2 (April, 1981):165–95.

Hu, C. T. *The Education of National Minorities in Communist China*. Washington, D.C.: U.S. Government Printing Office, 1970.

Hudson, G. F. "The Nationalities of China." *St. Anthony's Papers*, No. 7 (1960):51–61.

Hudson-Edwards, Alan, and Garland D. Bills. "Intergenerational Language Shift in an Albuquerque Barrio," in Edward L. Blansitt and Richard V. Teschner, eds., *A Festschrift for Jacob Ornstein*. MA: Newbury House Publishers Inc., 1980:139–58.

Hughes, Christopher, *Switzerland*. New York: Praeger, 1975.

Hung-mao Tien. "Sinicization of National Minorities in China." *Current Scene* (November, 1974):1–14.

Hyer, Paul, and William Heaton. "The Cultural Revolution in Inner Mongolia." *The China Quarterly,* Vol. 36 (October–December, 1968):114–28.

The Important Documents of the First Plenary Session of the CPPCC. Peking: Foreign Language Press, 1955.

Jacobs, Jane. *The Question of Separatism: Quebec and the Struggle over Sovereignty.* New York: Random House, 1980.

Jaffe, A. J., Ruth M. Cullen, and Thomas D. Boswell. *The Changing Demography of Spanish Americans.* New York: Academic Press, Inc., 1980.

Jenkins Molieri, Jorge. *El Desafío Indígena en Nicaragua: El Caso de los Miskitos.* Mexico, D.F.: Editorial Katun, 1986.

Joy, Richard. *Languages in Conflict: The Canadian Experience.* Toronto: McClelland and Stewart, 1972 (originally published in 1967).

Kalbach, Warren. "Growth and Distribution of Canada's Ethnic Populations, 1891–1971," in Leo Driedger, ed., *The Canadian Ethnic Mosaic.* Toronto: McClelland and Stewart, 1978:82–104.

Kahn, Linda. "Social Change and Schooling in Quebec." Ph.D. dissertation, University of California, Berkeley, 1985.

Kallen, Horace. *Culture and Democracy in the United States.* New York: Boni and Liveright, 1924.

Kane, Tim. "Structural Change and Chicano Employment in the Southwest, 1950–1970: Some Preliminary Observations." *Aztlan* (Fall, 1973):383–98.

———. "Chicano Employment Patterns: An Analysis of the Effects of Declining Economic Growth Rates in Contemporary America." *Aztlan,* Vol. 10 (Fall, 1979):15–30.

Keech, William. "Linguistic Diversity and Political Conflict." *Comparative Politics,* Vol. 4, No. 3 (April, 1972):387–404.

Keefe, Susan. "Personal Communities in the City: Support Networks among Mexican-Americans and Anglo-Americans." *Urban Anthropology,* Vol. 9, No. 1 (Spring, 1980):51–74.

Kerr, Henry. *Switzerland: Social Cleavages and Partisan Conflict.* London: Sage Publications, 1974.

Korbin, F. E., and C. Goldscheider. *The Ethnic Factor in Family Structure and Mobility.* Cambridge, MA: Ballinger, 1978.

Kotov, K. F. *Autonomy of Local Nationalities in the Chinese People's Republic.* Translation of a 1959 Russian monograph. New York: Joint Publications Research Service, 1960.

Lal, Amrit. "Sinification of Ethnic Minorities in China." *Current Scene,* Vol. 8, No. 4 (February 15, 1970):1–25.

Laporte, Pierre-Etienne. "The Economic Impact of the Charter of the

French Language (Law 101)," in Calvin Veltman, ed., *Contemporary Quebec.* Montreal: Universite du Quebec a Montreal, 1981:150–161.

La Raza Unida Party in Texas. New York: Pathfinder Press, 1970.

Larson, Robert. "The White Caps of New Mexico: A Study of Ethnic Militancy in the Southwest." *Pacific Historical Review,* Vol. 22 (1975):171–85.

Law of Autonomy of the Atlantic Coast Regions of Nicaragua. Republic of Nicaragua, 1987.

League of United Latin American Citizens. *Resolutions: A Program for Domestic Equality, 1980.* Corpus Christi, TX: League of United Latin American Citizens, 1980.

Lee, Fu-Hsiang. "The Turkic Moslem Problem in Sinkiang: A Case Study of the Chinese Communists' Nationality Policy." Ph.D. dissertation, Rutgers University, 1973.

Lenin, V. I. *National Liberation, Socialism, and Imperialism: Selected Writings.* New York: International Publishers, 1968.

Levine, Charles. "Understanding Alinsky: Conservative Wine in Radical Bottles." *American Behavioral Scientist,* Vol. 17, No. 2 (November–December, 1973):279–84.

Levy, Jacques. *Cesar Chavez: Autobiography of La Causa.* New York: W. W. Norton, 1975.

Lieberson, Stanley. "The Impact of Residential Segregation of Ethnic Assimilation." *Social Forces,* Vol. 40 (1961):52–57.

———. *Language and Ethnic Relations in Canada.* New York: John Wiley & Sons, 1970.

Lieberson, Stanley, Guy Dalto, and Mary Ellen Johnston. "The Course of Mother-Tongue Diversity in Nations." *American Journal of Sociology,* Vol. 81, No. 1 (1975):34–61.

Lijphart, Arend. *Democracy in Plural Societies.* New Haven: Yale University Press, 1977.

Limon, Jose. "El Primer Congreso Mexicanista de 1911: A Precursor to Contemporary Chicanismo." *Aztlan* Vol. 5, Nos. 1 & 2 (Spring and Fall, 1974):85–117.

Liu Chun. *The National Question and Class Struggle.* Peking: Foreign Language Press, 1966.

Lopez, David E. "Chicano Language Loyalty in an Urban Setting." *Sociology and Social Research,* Vol. 62, No. 2 (January, 1978):267–78.

———. *Language Maintenance and Shift in the United States Today: The Basic Patterns and Their Social Implications. Volume III: Hispanics and Portuguese.* Los Alamitos, Calif.: National Center for Bilingual Research, 1982a.

———. *The Maintenance of Spanish over Three Generations in the United*

States. Los Alamitos, Calif.: National Center for Bilingual Research, 1982b.

Lopez, Manuel. "Patterns of Interethnic Residential Segregation in the Urban Southwest, 1960 and 1970," *Social Science Quarterly*, Vol. 62, No. 1 (March 1981):50–62.

Lortie, Pierre. "The New Entrepreneurial and Managerial Class in Quebec," in Calvin Veltman, ed., *Contemporary Quebec*. Montreal: Université du Quebec à Montréal, 1981:72–80.

"Los Afro-Nicaraguenses (Creoles) y la Revolucion." *WANI*, No. 4 (July–September, 1986):7–16.

Macias, Reynaldo. "National Language Profile of the Mexican-Origin Population in the United States," in Walker Conner, ed., *Mexican-Americans in Comparative Perspective*. Washington, D.C.: The Urban Institute Press, 1985:283–308.

Madrid, Arturo. "In Search of the Authentic Pachuco." *Aztlan*, Vol. 4, No. 1 (Spring, 1972):31–60.

Marin, Marguerite. 'Protest in an Urban Barrio: A Study of the Chicano Movement." Ph.D. dissertation, University of California, Santa Barbara, 1980.

Martin, William. *Switzerland: From Roman Times to the Present.* New York: Praeger, 1971.

Martinez, Daniel. "Discutiendo la Autonomia: Se Va Despejando el Camino." *Pensamiento Propio*, Vol. 4, No. 32 (April, 1986):4–9.

Massey, Douglas. "Effects of Socioeconomic Factors on the Residential Segregation of Blacks and Spanish American in U.S. Urbanized Areas." *American Sociological Review*, Vol. 44 (December 1979a):1015–22.

————. "Residential Segregation of Spanish Americans in United States Urbanized Areas," *Demography*, Vol. 16, No. 4 (November, 1979b):553–63.

Massey, Douglas, and Brendan Mullan. "Processes of Hispanic and Black Spatial Assimilation." *American Journal of Sociology*, Vol. 89, No. 4 (1984):836–73.

Matre, Marc, and Tatcho Mindiola. "Residential Segregation in Southwestern Metropolitan Areas: 1970." *Sociological Focus*, Vol. 14, No. 1 (January, 1981):15-31.

Mayer, Kurt. "The Jura Problem: Ethnic Conflict in Switzerland." *Social Research*, Vol. 35, No. 4 (Winter, 1968):707–41.

McMillen, Donald. *Chinese Communist Power and Policy in Xinjiang, 1949–1977.* Boulder, Colo.: Westview Press, 1979.

McRae, Kenneth. *Switzerland: Example of Cultural Coexistence.* Toronto: The Canadian Institute of International Affairs, 1964.

————. "Empire, Language, and Nation: The Canadian Case," in S. N.

Eisenstadt and Stein Rokkan, eds., *Building States and Nations: Analyses by Region, Vol. II.* Beverly Hills, CA: Sage Publications, 1973.

McRoberts, Kenneth, and Dale Posgate. *Quebec: Social Change and Political Crisis.* Rev. ed. Toronto: McClelland and Stewart, 1980.

"Minority Nationalities in Communist China." *Current Background* (Hong Kong: American Consulate General), No. 430 (December 10, 1956).

Mirowsky, John, and Catherine Ross. "Language Networks and Social Status among Mexican Americans." *Social Science Quarterly,* Vol. 65, No. 2 (June, 1984):551–564.

Mittelbach, Frank, and Joan Moore. "Ethnic Endogamy: The Case of Mexican Americans." *American Journal of Sociology,* Vol. 74 (1968):50–62.

Mittelbach, Frank, Joan Moore, and Ronald McDaniel. *Intermarriage of Mexican-Americans.* Advance Report 6, Mexican-American Study Project. Los Angeles: Graduate School of Business Administration, University of California, 196.

Morrock, Richard. "Minority Nationalities in China." *Journal of Contemporary Asia Quarterly,* Vol. 2, No. 2 (1972):181–91.

Morton, W. L. "The Historical Phenomenon of Minorities: The Canadian Experience." *Canadian Ethnic Studies,* Vol. 13, No. 3 (1981):1–39.

Moseley, George. "China's Fresh Approach to the National Minority Question." *The China Quarterly* (October–December, 1965):15–27.

———. *The Party and the National Question in China.* Cambridge: The M.I.T. Press, 1966a.

———. *A Sino-Societ Cultural Frontier: The Ili Kazakh Autonomous Chou.* Monograph No. 22. Cambridge: Harvard University East Asian Research Center. 1966b.

———. "The Consolidation of the South China Frontier. Berkeley: University of California Press, 1973.

Munoz, Carlos, Jr., and Mario Barrera. "La Raza Unida Party and the Chicano Student Movement in California." *Social Science Journal,* Vol. 19, No. 2 (April, 1982):101–19.

Munoz, Carlos. "Youth, Identity and Power: The Chicano Generation." Unpublished manuscript, 1981.

Murguia, Edward. *Chicano Intermarriage: A Theoretical and Empirical Study.* San Antonio, TX: Trinity University Press, 1982.

Murguia, Edward, and Ralph Cazares. "Intermarriage of Mexican Americans," in G. A. Cretser and J. J. Leon, eds. *Intermarriage in the United States.* New York: Haworth Press, 1982, 91–100.

Murguia, Edward, and W. Parker Frisbie. "Trends in Mexican American

Intermarriage: Recent Findings in Perspective." *Social Science Quarterly*, Vol. 58, No. 3 (December, 1977):374–89.

Nabokov, Peter. *Tijerina and the Courthouse Raid*. Albuquerque: University of New Mexico, 1969.

"National Minorities: The Policy." *China News Analysis* (Hong Kong), No. 563 (May 7, 1965).

Navarro, Armando. "The Concept of La Raza Unida." Paper presented at a Raza Unida party conference, Riverside, California, 1972.

———. "The Evolution of Chicano Politics." *Aztlan*, Vol. 5, Nos. 1 and 2 (Spring and Fall, 1974):57–84.

———. "El Partido de La Raza Unida in Crystal City: A Peaceful Revolution." Ph.D. dissertation, University of California, Riverside, 1974.

———. "The Development of a New Concept." *Agenda*, Vol. 10, No. 5 (September–October, 1980):4–8.

Nevitte, Neil. "The Religious Factor in Contemporary Nationalism Movements: An Analysis of Quebec, Wales and Scotland," in Edward Tiryakian and Ronald Rogowski, eds., *New Nationalisms of the Developed West*. Boston: Allen & Unwin, 1985:337–52.

Nicarauac. Special issue on "La Costa Atlantica de Nicaragua" (Managua), October, 1982.

Nichols, James. "Minority Nationality Cadres in Communist China." Ph.D. dissertation, Stanford University, 1968.

———. "A Quantitative Perspective on Minority Cadres in Tibet." Paper delivered at the Asian Studies on the Pacific Coast Annual Conference, Eugene, Oregon, 1977a.

———. "Research Note: China's Minority Cadres." Manuscript, 1977b.

Nietschmann, Bernard. "Ecological Change, Inflation, and Migration in the Far Western Caribbean." *Geographical Review*, Vol. 69 (January, 1979):1–24.

Norwood, Susan, and Gerardo Zeledon. "Bilinguismo en la Costa Atlantica," *WANI*, No. 2–3 (December–May, 1985):14–21.

Olzak, Susan. "Ethnic Mobilization in Quebec." *Ethnic and Racial Studies*, Vol. 5, No. 3 (July, 1982):253–75.

Ortiz, Isidro. "Chicano Urban Politics and the Politics of Reform in the Seventies." Unpublished paper, 1984.

Ossenberg, Richard. "Colonialism, Language and False Consciousness: The Mythology of Nationalism in Quebec." *Canadian Review of Sociology and Anthropology*, Vol. 15, No. 2 (1978):145–47.

Padilla, Amado. "The Role of Cultural Awareness and Ethnic Loyalty in Acculturation," in Amado Padilla, ed., *Acculturation*. Boulder, Colo.: Westview Press, 1980:47–84.

Padilla, Felix. "On the Nature of Latino Ethnicity." *Social Science Quarterly*, Vol. 65, No. 2 (1984):651–64.

Pao-chien Tseng. "Language and National Unity: China," in William Beer and James Jacob, eds., *Language Policy and National Unity*. Totowa, N.J.: Rowman & Allanheld:178–97.

Parenteau, Roland. "The Role of State Corporations in Quebec's Economic Development," in Calvin Veltman, ed., *Contemporary Quebec*. Montreal: Université du Quebec à Montréal, 1981:45–55.

Penalosa, Fernando. *Chicano Sociolinguistics*. Rowley, Mass.: Newbury House Publishers, 1980.

Penalosa, Fernando, and Edward McDonagh. "Social Mobility in a Mexican-American Community." *Social Forces*, Vol. 44 (June, 1966):498–505.

Pinard, Maurice, and Richard Hamilton. "The Parti Quebecois Comes to Power: An Analysis of the 1976 Quebec Election." *Canadian Journal of Political Science*, Vol. 11, No. 4 (December, 1978):739–75.

Piotte, Jean-Marc, and Pauline Vaillancourt. "Toward Understanding the Enigmatic Parti Quebecois." *Synthesis*, Vol. 11, No. 4 (Fall, 1978):35–52.

Pipes, Richard. *The Formation of the Soviet Union: Communism and Nationalism, 1917–1923*. Rev. ed. Cambridge: Harvard University Press, 1964.

Pitt, Leonard. *The Decline of the Californios: A Social History of the Spanish-Speaking Californians, 1846–1890*. Berkeley: University of California Press, 1966.

Plascencia, Luis. "Low Riding in the Southwest: Cultural Symbols in the Mexican Community," in Mario Garcia et al., eds., *History, Culture, and Society*. Ypsilanti, Mich.: Bilingual Press, 1983:141–75.

Plotkin, Sidney. "Democratic Change in the Urban Political Economy: San Antonio's Edwards Aquifer Controversy," in David Johnson, John A. Booth, and Richard Harris, eds., *The Politics of San Antonio*. Lincoln: University of Nebraska Press, 1983:157–174.

Porter, John. *The Vertical Mosaic*. Toronto: University of Tornoto Press, 1965.

———. "Ethnic Pluralism in Canadian Perspective," in Nathan Glazer and Daniel Moynihan, eds., *Ethnicity: Theory and Experience*. Cambridge: Harvard University Press, 1975.

Pruger, Robert, and Harry Specht. "Assessing Theoretical Models of Community Organization Practice: Alinsky As a Case in Point," *The Social Service Review*, Vol. 43, No. 2 (June, 1969):123–35.

Pye, Lucien. "China: Ethnic Minorities and National Security," in Nathan

Glazer and Daniel Moynihan, eds., *Ethnicity: Theory and Experience.* Cambridge: Harvard University Press, 1975:489–512.

Quesenberry, Stephen, and Roxanne Dunbar Ortiz. "Indigenous Rights, Human Rights and Autonomy: The Miskitu People in Nicaragua." Unpublished paper, 1986.

Raynauld, Andre. "The Quebec Economy: A General Assessment," in Dale Thomson, ed., *Quebec Society and Politics: Views from the Inside.* Toronto: McClelland and Stewart, 1973:139–53.

Report of the Royal Commission on Bilingualism and Biculturalism, Book 9. Canadian Government Publications Center. Ottawa: Queens Printer, 1965–1971.

Republic of Nicaragua. *The Philosophy and Policies of the Government of Nicaragua* (March, 1982).

Rioux, Marcel. "The Development of Ideologies in Quebec," in Richard Schultz, Orest Kruhlak, and John Terry, eds., *The Canadian Political Process.* 3d ed. Toronto: Holt, Rinehard and Winston, 1979:98–113.

Rocha, Rodolfo. "The Influence of the Mexican Revolution on the Mexican-Texas Border, 1910–1916." Ph.D. dissertation, Texas Tech University, 1981.

Rodriguez, Sylvia. "The Hispano Homeland Debate." Working Paper Series No. 17. Stanford, Calif.: Stanford Center for Chicano Research, October 1986.

Romero, Mary. "Las Gorras Blancas, A Class Struggle Against the Transformation of Land Ownership and Usage in Northern New Mexico." Papers presented at the Annual Meeting of the Western Social Science Association, San Diego, California, 1981.

Rosaldo, Renato. "Assimilation Revisited." Working Paper Series No. 9. Stanford, Calif.: Stanford Center for Chicano Research, July, 1985.

Rosenbaum, Robert. "Las Gorras Blancas of San Miguel County, 1889–1890," in Renato Rosaldo, Robert Calvert, and Gustav Seligmann, eds., *Chicano: The Evolution of a People.* Minneapolis: Winston Press, 1973.

———. *Mexicano Resistance in the Southwest.* Austin: University of Texas Press, 1981.

Sagarin, Edward, and James Moneymaker. "Language and Nationalist, Separatist, and Secessionist Movements," in Raymond Hall, ed., *Ethnic Autonomy—Comparative Dynamics.* New York: Pergamon Press, 1979:18–37.

Salgado de Snyder, Nelly, and Amado Padilla. "Cultural and Ethnic Maintenance of Interethnically Married Mexican Americans," *Human Organization,* Vol. 41, No. 4 (Winter, 1982):359–62.

Sanchez, Rosaura. *Chicano Discourse: Socio-historic Perspectives.* Rowley, Mass.: Newbury House Publishers, 1983.

Sandos, James. "The Plan of San Diego: War and Diplomacy on the Texas Border, 1915–1916." *Arizona and the West* (Spring, 1972):5–24.

Sandoval, Moises. *Our Legacy: The First Fifty Years.* Washington, D.C.: League of United Latin American Citizens, 1979a.

———. "The Struggle within Lulac." *Nuestro* (September, 1979b):30–32.

San Miguel, Guadalupe. "The Origins, Development, and Consequences of the Educational Segregation of Mexicans in the Southwest," in Eugene Garcia, Francisco Lomeli, and Isidro Ortiz, eds., *Chicano Studies: A Multidisciplinary Approach.* New York: Teachers College Press, 1984.

Santillan, Richard. *La Raza Unida.* Los Angeles: Tlaquilo Publications, 1973.

———. "The Politics of Cultural Nationalism: El Partido de la Raza Unida in Southern California, 1969–1978." Ph.D. dissertation, Claremont Graduate School, 1978.

Schlesinger, Andrew. "Las Gorras Blancas, 1889–1891." *Journal of Mexican American History,* Vol. 1, No. 2 (1971):87–143.

Schmid, Carol. *Conflict and Consensus in Switzerland.* Berkeley: University of California, 1981.

Schmidt, Fred, and Kenneth Koford. "The Economic Condition of the Mexican-American," in Gus Tyler, ed., *Mexican-Americans Tomorrow.* Albuquerque: University of New Mexico, 1975:81–106.

Schoen, Robert, and Lawrence Cohen. "Ethnic Endogamy among Mexican American Grooms: A Re-analysis of Generational and Occupational Effects." *American Journal of Sociology,* Vol. 86 (1980):359–66.

Schoen, Robert, Verne E. Nelson, and Marion Collins. "Intermarriage among Spanish Surnamed Californians." *International Migration Review,* Vol. 12, No. 3 (Fall, 1978):359–69.

Schurmann, Franz. *Ideology and Organization in Communist China.* 2nd ed. Berkeley: University of California Press, 1968.

Schwarz, Henry. "Communist Language Policies for China's Ethnic Minorities: The First Decade." *The China Quarterly* (October–December, 1962):170–82.

———. "Policies and Administration of Minority Areas in Northwest China and Inner Mongolia, 1949–1959." Ph.D. dissertation, University of Wisconsin, 1963.

———. *Chinese Policies towards Minorities: An Essay and Documents.* Occasional Paper No. 2. Western Washington State College Program in East Asian Studies, 1971.

Sekul, Joseph. "Communities Organized for Public Service: Citizen Power and Public Policy in San Antonio," in David Johnson, John A. Booth, and Richard J. Harris, eds., *The Politics of San Antonio.* Lincoln: University of Nebraska Press, 1983:175–90.

Shabad, Theodore. *China's Changing Map.* Rev. ed. New York: Praeger, 1972.

Shaheen, Samad. *The Communist (Bolshevik) Theory of National Self-Determination.* The Hague: W. Van Hoeve, 1956.

Sheldon, Paul. "Community Participation and the Emerging Middle Class," in Julian Samora, ed., *La Raza: Forgotten Americans.* Notre Dame, Ind.: University of Notre Dame, 1966:125–57.

Shockley, John. *Chicano Revolt in a Texas Town.* Notre Dame, Ind.: University of Notre Dame Press, 1974.

Sierra, Christine. "From Barrio Organization to National Advocacy: The National Council of La Raza, 1965 to 1980." Paper presented at the Annual Meeting of the American Political Science Association, New York City, 1981.

———. "The Political Transformation of a Minority Organization: The Council of La Raza, 1965–1980." Ph.D. dissertation, Stanford University, 1982.

Skerry, Peter. "Neighborhood COPS." *The New Republic* (February 6, 1984):21–23.

Skrabanek, R. L. "Language Maintenance among Mexican-Americans." *International Journal of Comparative Sociology,* Vol. 11 (1970):272–82.

Smiley, Donald. "French-English Relations in Canada and Consociational Democracy," in Milton Esman, ed., *Ethnic Conflict in the Western World.* Ithaca, N.Y.: Cornell University Press, 1977:179–203.

———. *Canada in Question: Federalism in the Eighties.* 3d ed. Toronto: McGraw-Hill Ryerson Limited, 1980.

Smith, Anthony D. *The Ethnic Revival in the Modern World.* Cambridge: Cambridge University Press, 1981.

Smith, Michael. "The Aztlan Migrations of the Nahuatl Chronicles: Myth or History?" *Ethnohistory,* Vol. 31, No. 3 (1984):153–86.

Snipp, C. Mathew, and Marta Tienda. "New Perspectives on Chicano Intergenerational Occupational Mobility. *Social Science Journal,* Vol. 19, No. 2 (April, 1982):37–50.

Snow, Edgar. *Red China Today.* New York: Vintage Books, 1971.

Sole, Yolanda R. "Language Maintenance and Language Shift among Mexican American College Students." *Journal of the Linguistic Association of the Southwest,* Vol. 1, No. 1 (August, 1975):22–47.

Solinger, Dorothy. "Minority Nationalities in China's Yunan Province: Assimilation, Power, and Policy in a Socialist State." *World Politics*, Vol. 30, No. 1 (October, 1977):1–23.

Southern California Association of Governments. *Southern California: A Region in Transition*. Vol. 1, *Scenarios of Future Immigration and Ethnicity*. Los Angeles, December, 1984.

Stalin, Joseph. *Marxism and the National Question: Selected Writings and Speeches*. New York: International Publishers, 1942.

Steinberg, Jonathan. *Why Switzerland?* Cambridge: Cambridge University Press, 1976.

Steiner, Jurg. *Amicable Agreement Versus Majority Rule: Conflict Resolution in Switzerland*. Rev. and enlarged ed. Chapel Hill: University of North Carolina Press, 1974.

Steiner, Jurg, and Jeffrey Obler. "Does the Consociational Theory Really Hold for Switzerland?" in Milton Esman, ed., *Ethnic Conflict in the Western World*. Ithaca, N.Y.: Cornell University Press, 1977:324–42.

Swadesh, Frances. "The Alianza Movement: Catalyst for Social Change in New Mexico," in June Helm, ed., *Spanish-Speaking People in the United States*. Proceedings of the Annual Spring Meeting of the American Ethnological Society, 1968:162–77.

Takaki, Ronald. *Iron Cages: Race and Culture in Nineteenth-Century America*. New York: Alfred A. Knopf, 1979.

Taylor, Paul. *Mexican Labor in the United States: Imperial Valley*. Vol. 6, No. 1. Berkeley: University of California Publications in Economics, 1928.

Teeple, Gary, ed. *Capitalism and the National Question in Canada*. Toronto: University of Toronto, 1972.

Teske, Raymond and Bardin Nelson. "An Analysis of Status Mobility Patterns among Middle-Class Mexican Americans in Texas." Ph.D. dissertation, Texas A&M University, 1973.

————. "An Analysis of Differential Assimilation Rates among Middle-class Mexican Americans." *The Sociological Quarterly*, Vol. 17 (Spring, 1976):218–35.

Texas Department of Health, Population Data System. *State Health Planning and Resource Department*, July 17, 1985.

Texas Raza Unida Party: A Political Action Program for the '70s, n.d., n.p.

Theriault, George. "Separatism in Quebec," in Raymond Hall, ed., *Ethnic Autonomy—Comparative Dynamics*. New York: Pergamon Press, 1979:102–36.

Thompson, Roger. "Language Loyalty in Austin, Texas: A Study of a Bilingual Neighborhood." Ph.D. dissertation, University of Texas, Austin, 1971.

Thurer, Georg. *Free and Swiss.* London: Oswald Wolff, 1970.

Tienda, Marta, and Lisa Neidert. "Language, Education, and the Socio-economic Achievement of Hispanic Origin Men." *Social Science Quarterly,* Vol. 65, No. 2 (June, 1984):519–36.

Tijerina, Reies Lopez. *Mi Lucha por la Tierra.* Mexico City, Mex.: Fondo de Cultural Economica, 1978.

Tinker, John. "Intermarriage and Assimilation in a Plural Society: Japanese-Americans in the United States," in G. A. Cretser and J. J. Leon, eds., *Intermarriage in the United States.* New York: Haworth Press, 1982, 61–73.

Tirado, Miguel. "Mexican American Community Political Organization." *Aztlan,* Vol. 1, No. 1 (Spring, 1970):53–78.

———. "The Mexican American's Participation in Voluntary Political Associations." Ph.D. dissertation, Claremont Graduate School, 1970.

Tiryakian, Edward, and Neil Nevitte. "Nationalism and Modernity," in Edward Tiryakian and Ronald Rogowski, eds., *New Nationalisms of the Developed West.* Boston: Allen & Unwin, 1985:57–86.

Torres, Louis. "East Los Angeles Neighborhoods Unite." *Nuestro* (August 1980):23.

Trofimenkoff, Susan Mann. *The Dream of Nation: A Social and Intellectual History of Quebec.* Toronto: Gage Publishing, 1983.

Union Research Service. (Hong Kong: Union Research Institute.) Vol. 30, No. 21 (1963).

Valdez, Avelerdo. "Recent Increases in Intermarriage by Mexican American Males: Bexar County, Texas, from 1971 to 1980," *Social Science Quarterly,* Vol. 64, No. 1 (March, 1983):136–44.

Valdez, Dennis. *El Pueblo Mexicano en Detroit y Michigan: A Social History.* Detroit: Wayne State University, 1982.

Van Valey, Thomas, Keith Woods, and Wilfred Marston, "Patterns of Segregation among Hispanic-Americans: A Base-Line for Comparison." *California Sociologist,* Vol. 5, No. 2 (Summer, 1982):27–36.

Veltman, Calvin. "The Retention of Minority Languages in the United States," in Ronald Pedone, ed., *The Retention of Minority Languages in the United States.* Washington, D.C.: U.S. Government Printing Office, 1980:3–45.

———. *Contemporary Quebec.* Montreal: Departement d'études urbaines, Université du Quebec à Montréal, 1981.

Vigil, Maurilio. *Chicano Politics.* Washington, D.C.: University Press of America, 1977.

Vilas, Carlos. *The Sandinista Revolution: National Liberation and Social Transformation in Central America.* New York: Monthly Review Press, 1986.

Warburton, T. Rennie. "Nationalism and Language in Switzerland and

Canada," in Anthony Smith, ed., *Nationalist Movements*. London: Macmillan, 1976:88–109.

Wardhaugh, Ronald. *Language & Nationhood: The Canadian Experience*. Vancouver: New Star Books, 1983.

Weber, David, ed. *Foreigners in Their Native Land*. Albuquerque: University of New Mexico, 1973.

Weber, Henri. *Nicaragua: the Sandinista Revolution*. London: Verso Press, 1981.

Weeks, O. Douglas. "The League of United Latin-American Citizens: A Texas-Mexican Civic Organization." *Southwestern Political and Social Science Quarterly*, Vol. 10 (December, 1929):257–78.

Wilde, Margaret. "The Sandinistas and the Costeños." *Caribbean Review*, Vol. 10, No. 4 (1981):8–11, 44.

Wise, David. *The Politics of Lying*. New York: Vintage Books, 1973.

Woods, Sister Frances. *Mexican Ethnic Leadership in San Antonio*. Washington, D.C.: The Catholic University of America Press, 1949.

Yih, Katherine. "Distribuición Etnica en la Estructura Económica y Política de la Zona Especial II." *Encuentro*, No. 24–25 (April–September, 1985):103–15.

Yih, Katherine, and Alice Slate. "Bilingualism on the Atlantic Coast." *WANI*, No. 2–3 (December–May, 1985):23–26, 55–56. (WANI is a journal published by CIDCA, the Centro de Investigaciones y Documentacion de la Costa Atlantica, in Managua.)

Zeleny, Carolyn. *Relations between Spanish-Americans and the Anglo-Americans in New Mexico*. Ph.D. dissertation, Yale University, 1944. Reprinted by Arno Press, 1974.

Ziegler, Jean. *Switzerland: The Awful Truth*. New York: Harper & Row, 1979 (originally published 1976).

Index

202   *Index*

Cortez, Gregorio, 10
Costeños, 149, 151–52
Court of Private Land Claims, 13
Creoles, 140–42, 146, 153
crosscutting cleavages, 138
Crusade for Justice, 37, 45
Crystal City, TX, 34, 39–40
Cuba, 53
Cubans in Nicaragua, 146
"cultural division of labor," 89
cultural nationalism, 196; Chicano,
    46–48; Plan de Santa Barbara,
    42–43
Cuyamel Fruit Company, 143
CVP. *See* Christian Democratic
    Party

Dallas, TX, 71
decentralization, 123, 125, 129–30,
    138
*Declaration of Principles of the
    Popular Sandinista Revolution in
    Regards to the Indigenous Com-
    munities of the Atlantic Coast*,
    152–53
"democratic centralism," 54
Democratic party, 13, 28, 31
Denver, CO, 3–4, 37, 71
Denver Youth Conferences (Na-
    tional Chicano Youth Liberation
    Conference), 37, 39, 41, 171
Detroit, 83n
discrimination, 67–68
Dunn, James, 130–31
Duplessis, Maurice, 90

Eastern Europe, 51
East Los Angeles, 60–61
Edinburg, TX, 79
education: Chicano, 41–44, 70
El Paso, TX, 40, 60, 76
Engels, Frederick, 120

English language, 22–24, 140, 175,
    212; Canada, 86; Caribbean dia-
    lect, 140; Chicano, 72–78; "En-
    glish only" movement, 158,
    172–75
Esteli, 138
European stock in Nicaragua, 139–
    40
explicit regional autonomy, 160–63

Fagoth, Steadman, 146–47
FBI, 53
FDP. *See* Free Democratic Party
Federal Pact, 128
FLJ. *See* Front de liberacion juras-
    sienne
Floyd, Mary Beth, 74
FLQ. *See* Front pour la Liberacion
    du Québec
Fonseca, Carlos, 144
Ford Foundation, 56
Fort Worth, TX, 60
France, 123, 127, 136
Francophone "sovereignty-associa-
    tion," 162, 164
fraternal insurance societies. *See*
    mutual aid societies
Free Democratic Party (FDP), 125
Free Speech movement, 34
French language, 87–89, 96–98,
    124, 128, 131–35, 138, 174
Fribourg, 124, 127–28
Front de liberacion jurassienne,
    135
Front pour la Liberacion du Qué-
    bec (FLQ), 91
FSLN (Sandinista Front for Na-
    tional Liberation), 144–45, 150–
    51

"gabacho," 37, 43
Galarza, Ernesto, 56

ABOUT THE AUTHOR

MARIO BARRERA is professor of ethnic studies at the University of California, Berkeley, and the author of *Race and Class in the Southwest* (1979). He received his Ph.D. in political science from Berkeley in 1970, and was one of the founders of the National Association for Chicano Studies in 1973.